On Responsibility: The Moving Image Questions Spectatorship

Edited by
Lorenzo Lazzari

Adriatico Book Club
Grafiche Veneziane
Università Iuav di Venezia

How might the moving image offer a right of reply, or rather a responsibility? In his "Requiem for the Media" Jean Baudrillard argues, outside the psychological or moral sphere, that responsibility amounts to the reciprocity of "a speech and a response," that is, the establishment of a common space that allows, "on the basis of an antagonistic reciprocity,"[1] the flourishing of communication which is understood as a fair symbolic exchange between beings. The aforementioned short essay was published in the early 1970s, a key historical moment in which criticism of mass media society—especially television—had come of age.

This was in the wake of texts by the likes of Guy Debord, Hans Magnus Enzensberger, Marshall McLuhan and Gene Youngblood—concurrently with counter-cultural publications such as *Guerrilla Television* or *Radical Software* by Michael Shamberg and the Raindance Corporation.[2] Despite the multifaceted positions and arguments around the

1 Jean Baudrillard, "Requiem for the Media," in *For a Critique of the Political Economy of the Sign*, trans. Charles Levin (St. Louis: Telos Press, 1981), 169–170, orig. pub. *Pour une critique de l'economie politique du signe*, (Paris: Éditions Gallimard, 1972).

2 I refer to: Guy Debord, *The Society of the Spectacle*, trans. Donald Nicholson-Smith (New York: Zone Books, 1994), orig. pub. *La société du spectacle* (Paris: Buchet-Chastel, 1967); Hans Magnus Enzensberger, "Constituents of a Theory of the Media," trans. Stuart Hood, in *The Consciousness Industry: On Literature, Politics and the Media*, ed. Michael Roloff (New York: A Continuum book-The Seabury Press, 1974); Marshall McLuhan, *Understanding Media: The Extensions of Man* (New York: McGraw-Hill, 1964); Raindance Corporation (ed.), *Radical Software* 1, nos. 1–4 and *Radical Software* 2, nos. 1–6, (1970–1974); Michael Shamberg and Raindance Corporation, *Guerrilla Television* (New York: Rinehart & Winston Holt, 1971); Gene Youngblood, *Expanded Cinema* (New York: E. P. Dutton & Co.,1970).

feasibility of using the televisual media as a revolutionary tool, all the contributors seemed to agree on one point at least: "In the age of television, politics is conducted through media-generated icons designed to manufacture consent."[3] Baudrillard's position, explicitly in contrast with Enzensberger's, is that this media *agency* is not due to its content but to its own form, to its structure which intrinsically abstracts, separates and abolishes exchange by instituting social division.[4]

However, what might be understood as "separation" means something radically different to Debord and to Baudrillard. For the former, it signifies the operation through which the spectacle acts, moving the spectator away from life and thus activating an independent representation—an image unrelated to people's activities and intended only for the production and consumption of desire. A distance is thus discerned and that fosters alienation. For the latter, on the other hand, separation is the structural impossibility to respond to a word, not bound by any distance between the communicants but by the code in which the message is transcribed in order to enter into the transmission–reception circuit, thus preventing these terms from responding to each other. Indeed, Baudrillard lays bare the implausibility of revolutionizing the media with any content whilst operating within this system and proclaims that the only conceivable revolution in the media would be

3 David Joselit, *Feedback: Television Against Democracy* (Cambridge-London: The MIT Press, 2007), XI.

4 Baudrillard, "Requiem for the Media," 166–169.

one which is capable of unhinging the non-communicative structure of the media itself.[5]

With the irresponsibility of mass media transmission, communication is withdrawn from the sphere of use. Subverting this structure, this obligation of language rendered inoperative by its code, means operating according to what Agamben would come to call profanation: "[...] to open the possibility of a special form of negligence, which ignores separation or, rather, puts it to a particular use."[6] Here separation is subtraction—of an object, a space, an action—from the sphere of common use in order to relegate it to the field of the sacred and thus of the unusable. According to Jacques Derrida, it is a question of inventing strategies within the sphere of mass media to "reorient the discourse, propose new rules [...] in order to restart the contract on different terms."[7]

While preparing for their 2017 exhibition at Treize, Paris, curators Sibylle de Laurens and Pascaline Morincôme interviewed eight members of Videofreex, one of the pioneering US collectives

5 Baudrillard offers two examples in this regard. The first is that employed by poetic language, in which terms, beyond the distinction between signifier and signified, respond to each other: a rejoinder which is "ultimately decontructive of all codes, of all control and power." The second example is that of transgressing advertising discourse through graffiti, as an "instantaneous deconstruction of the dominant discursive code." Baudrillard, "Requiem for the Media," 180–184.

6 Giorgio Agamben, *Profanations*, trans. Jeff Fort (New York: Zone Books, 2007), 75, orig. pub. *Profanazioni* (Rome: Nottetempo, 2005).

7 Jacques Derrida and Bernard Stiegler, *Echographies of Television: Filmed Interviews* (Cambridge-Oxford: Polity Press-Blackwell Publishers, 2002), 58, orig. pub. *Échographies de la télévision: Entretiens filmés* (Paris: Éditions Galilée, 1996).

who utilized video as a means of participatory representation of a community, running for a decade from the late-1960s. Unlike film, video, which started to become more accessible with the first Sony Portapaks from 1967, guaranteed an immediate visual feedback on a monitor of what the camera was observing. Thus the operation of creating the representation was no longer the sole privilege of one, but now included the community of people around the video-maker, including those who were recorded: they were not only seen but *seen seeing*. Moreover, recording on a half-inch tape, which was both more economical than film stock plus was graced with being able to be recorded over innumerable times, also allowed for the decentralization of production and distribution structures, at the same time remaining "completely outside of the influence of TV while still appearing as 'television' on TV sets,"[8] thus subverting the structure of the media itself.

In 1971, after their preliminary try-outs, Videofreex moved their base from New York City to Lanesville, a small town in the Catskill Mountains. There they setup a pirate community television station which ran until 1978 and was broadcast throughout Lanesville, occupying Channel 3's frequencies. The interview unravels this experiment in which, through the use of video and auxiliary equipment, that division between public and private became

8 Kris Paulsen, "Half-Inch Revolution: The Guerrilla Video Tape Network," Amodern, accessed December 18, 2019, http://amodern.net/article/half-inch-revolution.

blurred. Television typically acts as an undemocratic device for privatizing political life and denying the public sphere, whereas *Lanesville TV* represents, albeit just on a local community scale, the democratic struggle against that privatization process.

The principle of feedback, of immediate retroaction in real time of what the camera sees, has long been acknowledged as the advantage of video technology. However, the ingenuity by experimental film-makers to do the same in the field of film has not been lacking. In "Delay of Gratification" Enrico Camporesi spotlights *Production Stills* (1970) by Morgan Fisher and *Film Feedback* (1974) by Tony Conrad. In these two pieces the film-making apparatus becomes active within the production of the works themselves, not only intervening instrumentally within the technical process, but it becomes verified, as an agent of reflection upon its own nature, triggering paradoxical consequences regarding the position of the spectator as well. In Fisher's film, the spectator is not really contemplated as part of the construction of the depiction, but only called on as a plausible recipient of a *mise en abyme* setup, in which the only issue seems to be an awareness of the materiality from which the film projection originates. In contrast, Conrad underlines the processes of impression, development and fixing of the film in order to make the apparatus literally look at itself, in a combination such that the cameraman observes what the protectionist is projecting, which is actually what the cameraman is observing, in an intricate loop that unwinds and rewinds on itself, reducing the space-time interval that separates the moment of shooting from that of projection.

"Distance is not an evil to be abolished, but the normal condition of any communication,"[9] affirms Jacques Rancière, for whom the distance of the viewer must not be an unbridgeable gap that separates the one who knows from the one who doesn't, but rather that measure that allows both to verify knowledge by learning something, a third element, which both are not yet knowledgeable about. The spectator's emancipation "begins when we challenge the opposition between viewing and acting; when we understand that the self-evident facts that structure the relations between saying, seeing and doing themselves belong to the structure of domination and subjection. It begins when we understand that viewing is also an action that confirms or transforms this distribution of positions."[10] Vera Dika, in "*BLKNWS* and Response-Ability," describes the "crucial displacement" staged by Kahlil Joseph during the 2019 Venice Biennale in order to make visible a significant spectatorial absence: that of the American black community. Whoever possesses the privileges to be able to visit the international art exhibition and see Joseph's *BLKNWS* installation, is confronted "with a racial, ethnic, and economic divide," inherent in the art

9 Jacques Rancière, *The Emancipated Spectator*, trans. Gregory Elliott (London-New York: Verso, 2009), 10, orig. pub. *Le spectateur émancipé* (Paris: La Fabrique éditions, 2008).

10 Rancière, *The Emancipated Spectator*, 13.

system, which excludes bodies that aren't part of that sphere—predominantly white—of the observer. Joseph's work thus accentuates a sharp segregation between the viewer who sees and the bodies of those who *aren't able to see*—since they are not present—but who are in fact the object of representation: from the images they *watch* whilst they are looked at, naming and rendering so visible their "uncounted" bodies.[11] Dika's essay concludes with a third element, namely the letters that her students at New Jersey City University—almost all belonging to the black and Latino communities—sent to Joseph, thus furnishing a further possibility of reply.

"The word 'emancipation' means," continues Rancière, "the blurring of the boundary between those who act and those who look; between individuals and members of a collective body."[12] The exploits of film-makers Vittorio De Seta and Éric Baudelaire, recounted by Malvina Borgherini in "Mirroring in a Movie," challenge the boundaries between representation and action, on occasion generating a two-way relationship with the subject being filmed: an "observing through a lens the eyes that allow others to see you" she explicates. In *The Forgotten* (*I dimenticati*, 1959) De Seta gains access to the remote inhabitants of Alessandria del Carretto in Calabria where he begins to film the ancestral spring ritual known as *Festa dell'Abete*

11 See Jacques Rancière, *Disagreement: Politics and Philosophy*, trans. Julie Rose (Minneaopolis-London: University of Minnesota Press, 1999), orig. pub. *La Mésentente: Politique et philosophie* (Paris: Éditions Galilée, 1995).

12 Rancière, *The Emancipated Spectator*, 19.

(fir-tree festival). His is a work of representation, but not one intended for an extraneous gaze only—for the eyes of those that don't yet know, surveying anthropologically—but is held up like a mirror at the very moment those same eyes that had been filmed are able to attest each other in the projected images, immediately conferring a realization of being a culture, of constituting a community in itself. In *A Dramatic Film* (*Un film dramatique*) Éric Baudelaire exemplifies that same constitutive operation by making reference to the continuous intersection between private and public life—over four years—in an exchange project with a small group of youngsters from the Dora Maar middle school in banlieue Saint-Denis, northern Paris.

Each of these works, examined by the various authors here, questions the responsive dimension in which the viewer finds themself. None attempt to cancel or disregard the viewer's presence. What is questioned, what these moving images invite one to reflect upon, is the very status of spectatorship, especially when the gap becomes apparent, with no way to bridge it and make it back; the situation in which symbolic exchange is rendered inoperative. The various works highlighted in this volume challenge this distancing, offering a critical reflection to the thwarted exchange. It is therefore not a question of whether that distance itself ought to be dissolved, or any separation between the moving image and the spectator erased. Rather it is one of verifying to what *measure* it might be admissible, as spectators, to move within that distance that separates us from the work, and to investigate what that particular use might be, what the moving image might be capable of, conceivably of a separation that is able to bring back, to respond and thus to communicate.

Lorenzo Lazzari

LANESVILLE TV BROADCAST SYSTEM
c. 1975

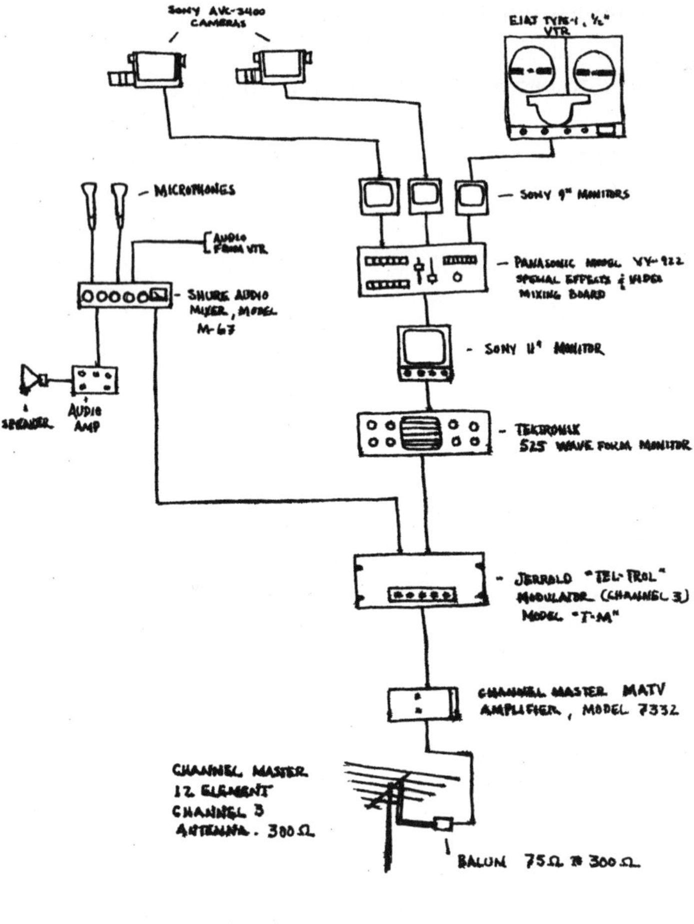

Videofreex, *Lanesville TV Broadcast System*, ca.1975. Photocopy, 21 × 29.7 cm.
Courtesy of Videofreex.com.

Interview With the Videofreex

Sibylle de Laurens and Pascaline Morincôme

In August 2015 we travelled through New York State to meet the Videofreex members and look at their personal archives. We recorded individual interviews of Skip Blumberg and Ann Woodward in New York City, and then went Upstate to visit Parry Teasdale and Carol Vontobel in their house at Chatham, and Bart Friedman in Saugerties. The recorded interviews that we brought back from our trip were edited together with emails and Skype conversations with Nancy Cain, Davidson Gigliotti and Mary Curtis Ratcliff from Videofreex and Abina Manning and Tom Colley from Video Data Bank. A first version of this interview was published as a sort of exhibition guide for the Videofreex retrospective that we organized in the Parisian alternative space Treize in January 2017. This re-edited version was made possible thanks to the friendly help of Deborah Birch and Videofreex.com.[1]

Sibylle de Laurens and Pascaline Morincôme: At the end of the 1960s and during the 1970s, different video groups began to appear, like Raindance Cor-

1 Videofreex.com is the new organizational name of the early video group Videofreex. Further information can be found on the website https://videofreex.com.

poration, Global Village and People's Video Theater. This was made possible partly by the introduction in the US of SONY's first video recorder, the Portapak. Videofreex was part of this "Videosphere."[2] How did you start to work as a collective?

Skip Blumberg: In 1967, Sony introduced this half-inch video for two markets: one was schools, the other was industry. I think tourism and other home uses were a third consideration, but artists and activists picked up the camera. There were all these little communities of people that applied video in different ways: some in the art world, some in music, some in business, some in schools, some in news and TV.

Mary Curtis Ratcliff: In 1969, David and I were living in New York and he had a camera.[3] He went to Woodstock,[4] and he came back with the camera and Parry. There is a saying in English that goes, "if you can't beat them, join them." So the three of us decided to start a group. We would just go and shoot anything that was of interest. Music, marches, etc.

S&P: One of the particularities of Videofreex in comparison to the other video groups at that time was that you first started to work

2 See Gene Youngblood, *Expanded Cinema* (New York: E. P. Dutton & Co., 1970), 260–264.

3 A newly introduced handheld video camera with microphone connected by a cable to the Portapak portable half-inch videotape recorder, altogether weighing 24 pounds.

4 The Woodstock Music and Art Fair, August 15–18, 1969.

for one of the biggest television networks in the US. The Videofreex—David, Parry and Mary Curtis—were chosen by CBS producer Don West to work on a new pilot program that he hoped would replace *The Smothers Brothers Comedy Hour*, a show the network judged too controversial.

Mary Curtis: Yes, it's how we became a group. All of a sudden there was too much work to do and we had to hire other people, so we took Nancy to Chicago with us. At that time she was working for CBS.[5]

Skip: Carol introduced me to the Videofreex. She and Nancy were friends before Videofreex ... they were roommates in uptown Manhattan. And when Nancy started working with Don West, the Videofreex needed help. So I left my job teaching and I started working with the Videofreex on the CBS project, in September or October of 1969.

Mary Curtis: We needed a technical person who really knew what to do and we found Chuck Kennedy. David met Davidson in a bank; he had a camera in his hand [*laughs*]! And then Bart came. We met Ann after CBS at an exhibition at Brandeis University[6] (MA).

Ann Woodward: Yes, I was a curatorial assistant as a student at the Rose Art Museum of

5 She was Don West's assistant producer.
6 The exhibition was held at the Rose Art Museum of Brandeis University (MA).

Brandeis University. The director was Russell Connor, who had been involved in the first broadcast television program about video art, at WGBH in Boston. He created the exhibition *Vision and Television*, which brought in a lot of video artists. This was Waltham, Massachusetts, in February 1970. Videofreex were part of that show. I had an offer to stay on at the museum through the summer and after that, I could either stay on working in the basement of the Rose Art Museum, which was pretty mundane, or I could do something more fun, like move to New York and get involved with the group. So that's what I did.

S&P: Paradoxically, you worked at CBS, a major TV network, in order to produce *Subject to Change*, which was about recording all the important events happening in the counterculture at that time. Why did you accept the job? You did an interview of one of the members of the Black Panther Party, Fred Hampton, who was killed by the police a couple of months after that. How did the Black Panther Party accept to make an interview with you as CBS reporters?

Mary Curtis: To tell the honest truth, although some people might not agree with this, we didn't have a lot of money. We were living on twenty-five dollars a week. But we did get money for a certain period of time ... it was only for five or six months ... from CBS. And it gave us the possibility to go to Chicago and to California. Because we couldn't afford that before. But it was difficult to be working for CBS and be part of the counterculture. There was a huge tension there. I remember in Chicago, we had talked to Abbie Hoffman and then we talked to William Kunstler.[7] We were in his office and Tom Hayden[8] was there too, and we were videotaping him. William Kunstler said "Are you working for someone?" and we said "Yes" ... and he said "Who are you working for?" We said "CBS" and he immediately said "Erase all the tape that you just made of me," and Parry just did exactly what he said and erased the tapes. We had to be honest with the Black Panthers and say we were working for CBS. But we said that we would make sure that CBS would not have this material, and that actually was what happened. Because we were up in the country in upstate New York in a farmhouse editing the video for *Subject to Change* and we read or heard on the radio that Fred Hampton was killed by the police. And then we were even more determined not to let CBS get those tapes. We finished the edit, we left the tapes up in the farmhouse and for some dumb reasons, we came back to Manhattan. They sent a private airplane or helicopter up to that same farmhouse and they stole those tapes of Fred Hampton and Abbie Hoffman.

7 William Kunstler was the lawyer of the Chicago Seven.
8 He was co-founder of Students for a Democratic Society.

Bart Friedman: CBS wanted to exploit our relationship with the counterculture. We were able to talk to people that would not talk to CBS. The executives were supposed to come down to our loft in SoHo to look at the result of our work. Don West wanted to add some CBS network footage about Fred Hampton's funeral. Parry said "You can't use that footage and if you try we won't do the show."[9]

Mary Curtis: After that, Skip and Parry went to the CBS building on 53rd Street with an empty guitar case and they got the tapes back. We really had to do that because we promised the Panthers, it was a point of honor that CBS would not hang on to those tapes and be able to do what they wanted to with it.

S&P: In 1969, you actually did present the *Subject to Change* pilot in your studio, the Videofreex loft, as a single channel TV show displayed on several monitors, in front of the CBS producers—and they refused the project. After that, you kept on doing screenings in your loft every week, which became known as the *Friday Night Screenings*. What was their concept?

Mary Curtis: Yes, that was after CBS. Because we were not the only group, there were many

9 "So Don, to his later regret, backed down and the live and videotape alternate culture/radical politics documentary and entertainment variety TV show went on in the Freex half-built Soho NYC studio, with the Videofreex in the control room. When finished, the execs, turning it down, said it was 'five years ahead of its time' and departed quickly." Skip Blumberg, email to the editor, January 25, 2020.

video groups and artists, and none of us could get on broadcast television and we wanted to show each other what we were doing. Videofreex had a loft on Prince Street, in SoHo, it was not yet SoHo, but it became SoHo. And we would invite everybody and by word of mouth it would get an audience. And we showed each other what we had videotaped and people would bring their tapes. It was around the same time as The Kitchen. At the time there were only three television stations in America, NBC, ABC, CBS. So what we were doing was really very different. We were recording the counterculture and none of their cameras were there. CBS was not there, nor ABC or NBC. We were hippies, we were inside the counterculture. All we had to do was point the camera in any direction. We just ran out with the equipment and videotaped whatever was happening. It was a real revolution in this country at that time.

S&P: At that time, the counterculture was intrinsically linked to the anti-war movements. Videofreex participated in the May Day protests, videotaping and sharing images of non-violent demonstrations and police violence, and edited a fifty-one minute tape as part of the Mayday Video Collective. You also recorded the Days of Rage in Chicago in 1969, the Women's Liberation March in New York in 1970, and documented how the movements organized themselves. What was your involvement in these political issues and your position during those demonstrations?

Mary Curtis: It was the position of wanting to record what was happening, none of us were in a political group. At that time there were groups of women, support groups for women about feminism, consciousness-raising, but none of us women in Videofreex were in those groups, for some reason. Nancy, Carol and I went to the Women's Strike for Equality in Manhattan, just to record what was going on and that was the reason to do it, just to record it.[10] Also it took us a while to figure out what was sexism. I grew up in the 1950s and so it was all very new, the idea of not only being a mother, a teacher, a nurse or a secretary, that there were other possibilities was a new idea. I was like twenty-six, twenty-seven, so I wished that I had gotten smarter earlier and been in that wonderful big march on the Fifth Avenue when all the thousands and thousands of women were there. What I tried to do is to give information through the *Curtis's Abortion* tape. In 1970, all of a sudden in the state of New York it was legal to have an abortion, for the first time ever. So I wanted to give the other women that information in case they needed it. So that was a radical thing to do. And I had hard times saying yes to do it and after that to have this tape restored because it was very very personal to me. But still I think it was a good thing to do. It was a risk that I took to get the information out.

10 The title of the half-inch open reel video is *Women's Lib Demonstration NYC.*

S&P: What was the link between this new politically involved video community, which considered itself as activist and the artistic avant-garde?

Ann: Videofreex is considered as an art group now, but it really wasn't. It was more political—news and information, "semi-documentaries," and getting the media out to the people.

Nancy Cain: I never thought I was making "art" when I picked up the video camera. I recorded events and talked intimately with people I met, and even though it was video to me, Barbara London—the first video curator at MoMA—would happily play the tapes; for example, a long portrait video of "Sharon" talking about her life as a battered woman and subsequent escape to freedom. As Barbara saw it, it was art. So it was art. There are many examples of this sort of video that have morphed from "things I did" and "things I saw" and "things that happened" into rarified moments in time that were thought of as art, by a certain crowd. There was the Freex loft, on Prince Street in 1970, with snazzy galleries springing up—some Freex related to them and liked to mingle with the serious high-priced art crowd and partake of the finest *hors d'œuvres*. Looking back it seems to me they were always two factions within the group, the "artists" and the "documentarians." But if there was an art show being produced by Freex, we would all participate.

Davidson Gigliotti: Elitism was the clear enemy, and the term was generally applied to government and institutions, but could also be applied to individuals who displayed arrogance or spoke from positions of authority. When one says radical, applied to American activists of the 1960s and 1970s, it doesn't mean that they were all Marxist scholars, readers of Sartre, Althusser, the Frankfurt School, Frederic Jameson, or Chairman Mao. Some had that knowledge, of course. But most of the people I knew were responding to the direct experience of America in the 1960s. They understood television. Most had never known a time without TV, and all had had certain shared experiences; grades K–12 in the 1950s, college in the 1960s, the Cuban Missile Crisis, the assassinations of the Kennedys and Martin Luther King, the Vietnam War, the Civil Rights Movement, Women's Liberation, the killings at Kent State College, the nightly news on NBC, ABC, and CBS. American radicalism of the 1960s grew, I believe, from these experiences. Regarding the establishment art scene, the Videofreex, Raindance, and the Ant Farm, were outsiders. During the 1960s the important writers and galleries were committed to Pop Art in painting. In sculpture Minimalism was ascendant. The nascent video community was never a consideration. An exception was Nam June Paik, who was a recognized artist in Europe, not so much as a video artist, but as a music composer and avant-garde performer. That helped, but even he was on the establishment fringes here in America. This is not to say that the art world was blind to video. But it was a matter of being properly credentialed. Bruce Nauman, for example, had the right credentials, an MFA from UC Davis, and an association with several important West Coast artists like William Wiley and Wayne Thiebaud. In 1968 he started working with video, using the hour-long tape format of the early CV studio decks to record certain durational performance pieces. Nauman was a recognized artist in the establishment art world. Leo Castelli gave him a show in New York featuring his videotapes in 1969. Videos by Joan Jonas, Vito Acconci, John Baldessari, Lynda Benglis, etc., soon appeared in the *Castelli-Sonnabend Videotapes and Films* catalogue. My point here is that video was OK if you were already a recognized artist whose work in other disciplines was known. The establishment art scene was not interested in Videofreex.

Skip: Some of us had art backgrounds. We had friends who were artists. We were invited to exhibit, we went to conferences and screenings in art museums, and we received art grants, but we were video-makers. We really saw ourselves as TV people. There was a development of video art in the art world that was contained. The art world was part of what we showed in, but we also showed in community centers, we were applying it as an activist

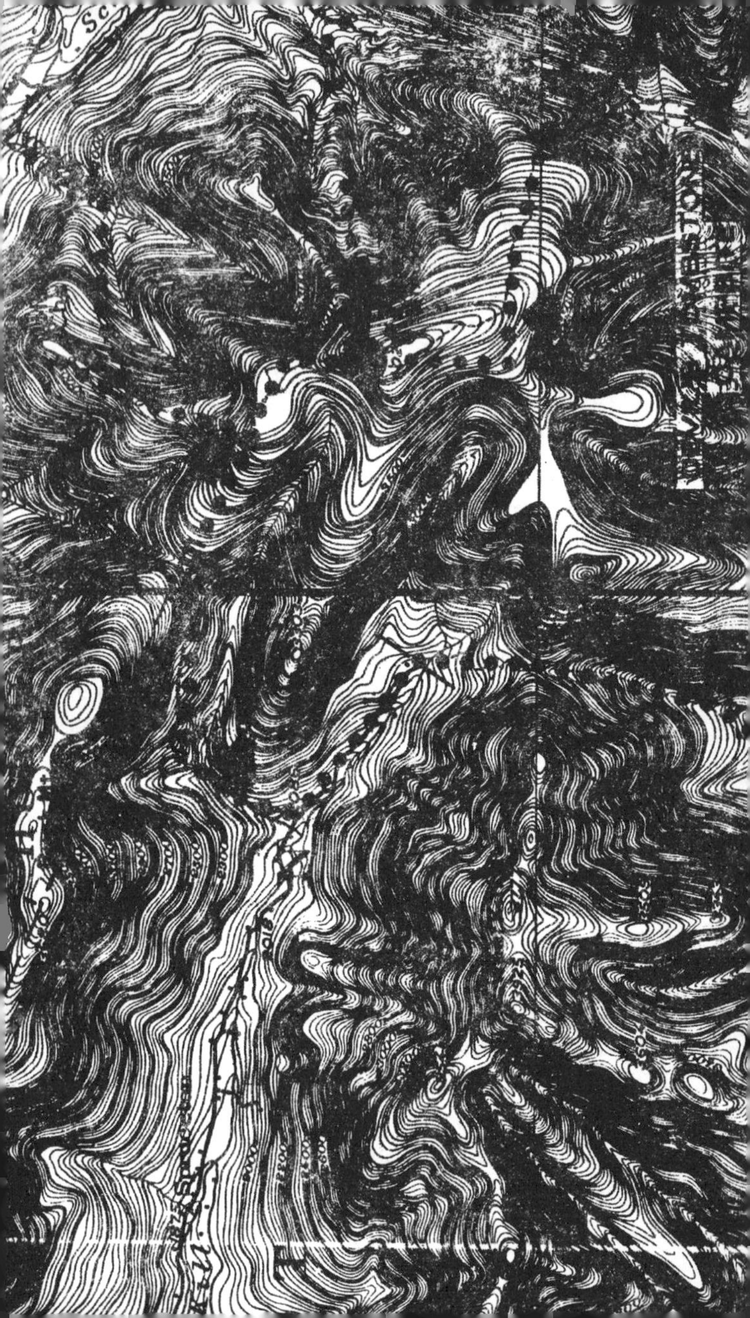

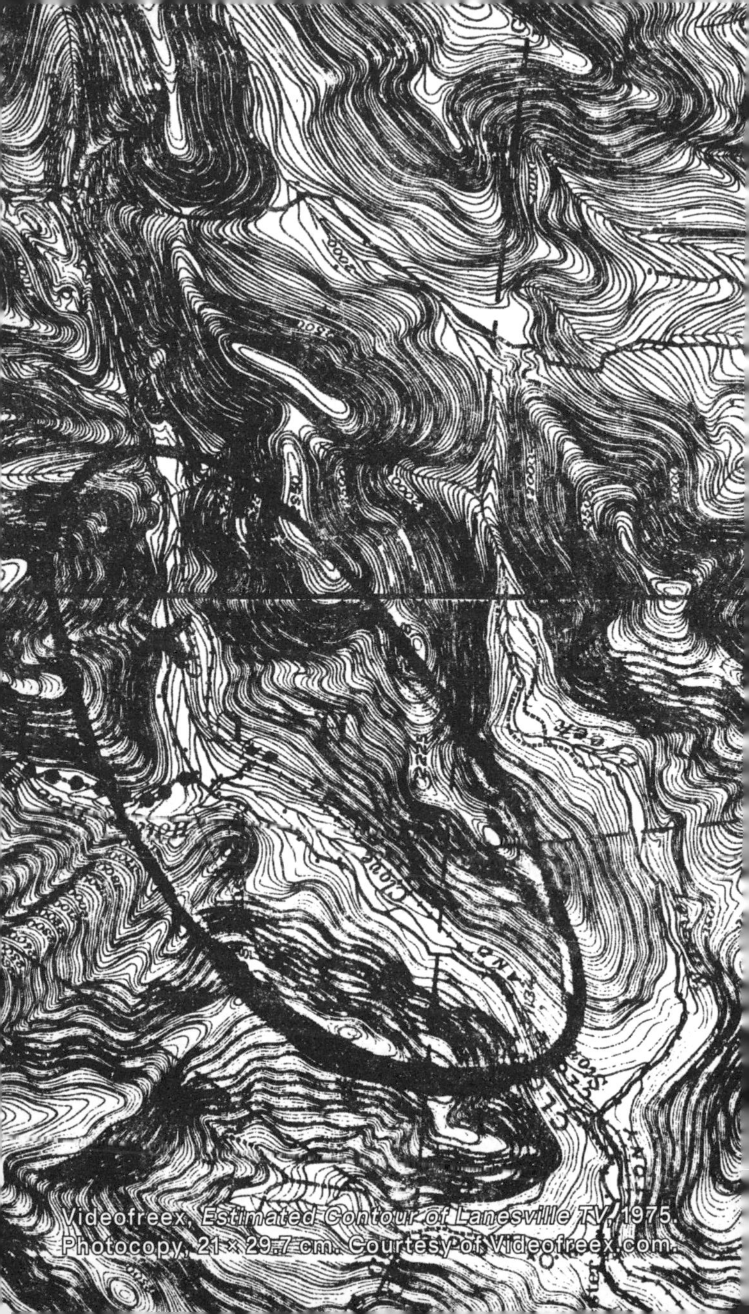

Videofreex, *Estimated Contour of Lanesville TV*, 1975. Photocopy, 21 × 29.7 cm. Courtesy of Videofreex.com.

tool; we were applying it in a lot of different forms. The video tools were created for a sort of home use and industrial use, but we saw that there could be television use. Television was a shared experience. Everybody watched at the same time. There was no instant replay at home; you had to watch it live. There was no VCR, there was no recording. It was like a shared community experience and very powerful for entertainment and news. Now there is time shifting, streaming television ... Some people don't watch television at all anymore—television will be obsolete some day soon. But the point is, the tools were not intended by Sony and the other manufacturers to be used to make television. We used it and we were rejected by the TV stations first because of vertical blanking, because of vertical sync ... if the 15,750 cycles per second frequency wasn't exactly right, the tapes wouldn't play properly on televisions receiving their signals (broadcast over the air through their TV's rabbit-ears antenna). So then the time-based error corrector was invented, which allowed our videos to go on broadcast television. It took our tapes' signal that was not exact, it locked it into a solid signal. It replaced vertical blanking with new vertical blanking that could be synced at the TV station. It kept the picture the same, but it replaced blanking and sync, so our work could be transmitted and seen by millions of people, even if Sony never intended it to be like that.

S&P: In 1971, Michael Shamberg, member of Raindance Corporation, published the founding text, *Guerrilla Television*,[11] about this generational movement of video makers that would produce a new kind of independent television with educational and social goals. The same year, you decided to leave New York to settle in the Catskill Mountains, in the small village of Lanesville where you produced your own independent and local TV programs with an unlicensed pirate low-power broadcast television station called *Lanesville TV*. You rented an old boarding house called Maple Tree Farm and turned it into a video center welcoming people interested in this new technology and organizing workshops all around the state. At that time, there were public programs which supported media centers in New York City, New York State and all over the US, such as the Experimental Television Center or the Alternate Media Center as well, and which gave you also the possibility to install an economy and to sustain the lives of your members.

Parry Teasdale: Yes, Governor Nelson Rockefeller set up the New York State Council of the Arts funding to grow from about a million or 2 million to 20 million in one year. And back then it was a huge amount ... and that created quite some controversy and the reason that we actually left to go upstate was because we realized with some good advice from people who knew about such things that the money was

11 Michael Shamberg and Raindance Corporation, *Guerrilla Television* (New York: Rinehart & Winston Holt, 1971).

going to be spread out over a lot of groups and there wasn't much going on upstate. It was necessity that drove us together. But when we worked together it worked very well because there was this shared understanding of the need for a group approach to make it happen. There were disagreements, actually there was not even a shared concept or political outlook but we had general agreements: we were all opposed to the war, we had nothing good to say about the Nixon administration and domestic policies, and we knew we were being spied on by the government.[12] At that time, everybody was experimenting with ways of making communities. Creating communities kind of instantly was perhaps an unrealistic expectation, anyway. But we had a community of interest where we could find people who were interested in using the same tools, but not for the same end. That made it distinctly different from having a dogma, an ideology.

Carol Vontobel: And we had a one-inch deck.

Parry: Well, yes, we had invested early on in that technology. And we had the ability to support it because we had a technical person working with us, Chuck Kennedy. Working with him we were able to make the equipment do a lot of things that it wasn't supposed to do and blend the portable cameras with multi-cameras systems or to do editing. The editing suite that we had was sophisticated for that time.

12 Maple Tree Farm was spied-on by the FBI.

It's primitive now but it would allow us to do clean electronic cuts and to insert pieces of video in other pieces of video in the editing process—that was really too expensive to do most anywhere else.

> Carol: And that's what we were funded to do, to teach people. That's how we got money from the State Council. I'm not exactly sure that we would have been able to keep the money some other way, so people came because of course we needed to do that.

Parry: And because we were interested in doing it. The thing was that our interests coincided with the interests of the whole community because everybody wanted to be able to make more refined work. And you couldn't do that with the tools as they were presented.

> Skip: People would come to Maple Tree Farm and stay for a while. People came from all around the US and the world, and we hosted them, with grants to pay for part of it, so we never charged our visitors.

Ann: And we did *The Spaghetti City Video Manual*.[13] Parry wrote it, I illustrated it, and Chuck was the kind of the technical consultant.

13 *The Spaghetti City Video Manual* was published in 1973. This technical guide presents the different tools used in the case of a video recording and editing as well as their maintenance guidelines. Videofreex, *The Spaghetti City Video Manual* (New York: Praeger Publishers, 1973).

S&P: Some other *media centers*, as dedicated places for video and technical democratization, controlled their own diffusion, and were running their own TV program on local or cable TV channels. Videofreex's economic strategy is interesting as you were working and living with the support of the state under the name of Media Bus, which at the same time gave you the possibility to run your own illegal TV channel. How did you technically start to produce *Lanesville* TV—as an illegal program?

Bart: We were hacking. "Hacking" became a popular notion a few years ago, so I use that word now and I apply it to the things we did when we started. We took a modulator that created a Channel 3 signal. When we bought the equipment there was a little portable RF unit in the battery compartment and this modulator would turn the video signal into a TV signal. You put a wire from the modulator to the terminals on the back of your television set and turn the channel selector to Channel 3 because the modulators were all Channel 3 and all televisions had a blank Channel 3. It was like a dead zone. So you plug it in and at the moment when the wire touches the terminal at the back of the TV set you get the Channel 3 signal. So we had one that was about the size of a big bread box and it was used, along with a signal amplifier, for transmitting our video signals from our rooftop antenna to the town.

Parry: Mainstream television had special-effects boards. They used them constantly in TV shows but they didn't do much with them. And they would use a switcher that could dissolve or fade out to black or fade up. Very quickly, Sony came out with something called the SEG 1, Special Effects Generator. It was a small little box with faders and switches for cameras. It was meant to be for little school systems, organizations or amateurs but it was meant to work with a little studio camera, so everybody would stand behind the tripod. That would be the miniaturization and the bargain basement version of a big TV studio. We didn't use cameras like that, we didn't put them on tripods, we liked to get them off, to walk around with the camera and to be engaged. So, we began to assemble what amounted to the equipment for TV production house but focus on the small equipment. And focus on mobile production, bringing it back to the studio and then blending it in some—either a live presentation or videotape programs that would include the editing. So we invested in one of those SEG 1 boxes very early on. And we were then able to do multi-camera television production. The one thing that we didn't really have a very good piece of equipment for was an intercom. In television it's all command and control, top-down approach to have you create something. CBS had given us these old telephone operator headsets—I guess they were still using it for television, but they never worked exactly right. We hated them, so we got rid of it. And then, if you had a good shot, the camera people and the action is really dictated by what was going on; it was chaotic, and it wasn't smooth, but it gives you a different sense, it was not some plotted script thing, it was spontaneous and that has good and bad aspects to it but it generated some excitement. The best of it was when, for instance, for the CBS show, we did the music. The music lends itself to fast cutting and fast switching and to people getting eye camera angles, so everyone who was doing the switching could work with the rhythm of the music but the camera was also working with the rhythm of the music and nobody was saying "Camera 2, get the guitar player, Camera 1 get the bass player, the drummer." It was much more spontaneous. I'm not saying we invented it, since there have been millions of hours produced for music videos and things, but it was a way of working that was different from what we had seen on television.

S&P: By recording these tapes—made in your living room or around the Lanesville community—you made use of your private sphere, with the political aim of spreading it around the public realm. We can consider these images and your engagement with intimacy as politicized images. There is something interesting going on regarding your audience, in the way that you involve them, in your political goals, and in your community. *Lanesville TV* programs were broadcast within just a few kilometers' radius.

Some of you experienced different scales of distribution during and after Videofreex, with TVTV for example, where the shoots were well organized; you were aired by important channels and networks (you actually had reviews in important local newspapers, national news, and cultural magazines). It was something really different from *Lanesville TV*, from your way of working with your local audience. How was the public involved in this alternate TV movement? What was your relationship with your audience?

Parry: The problem with video was there was not much of a way to play it to large audiences. You could gather people and set up a monitor, like set up your computer here and set up the video recorder and play tapes, but even if you invited people there wasn't a place or a mechanism to get it out. That's what was happening during that time. Cinema had a distribution system, they didn't belong to a union, maybe, but they were definitively organized, they were particularly effective all the time. They could get films out to campuses and to community groups where there were availabilities. And there was a lot of technology in place; the 16mm projector was ubiquitous in school. That is the problem we confronted and the solution was twofold. One is to first of all have this pirate television station not necessarily in the order of priority and the other was to train people how to do it for themselves so they could apply what they were doing to whatever mechanism, avenue or distribution became available to them. So sometimes there would even be public television stations although very infrequently. Mostly it was cable and sometimes it was community performances ... And then there was this group TVTV. I didn't really do the shooting but Skip, and Nancy and Bart were all very involved and Chuck was there too. They managed to get TV time but these, by video standards, were highly polished documentaries—look at the editing of the Republican and Democratic Convention in 1972.

Nancy: I'm amazed to find in answering this that it barely made a difference to me from delivery system to delivery system, from audience to audience. My concept of video did not change. The video was consistent. A wider audience does not change the way video is in my mind. Transitions in location and venue were for me pretty seamless. My POV shooting style improved a bit, but didn't change. *The Night Owl Show* in Woodstock was a logical progression from *Lanesville TV*. Programming was produced by community members who all had different ideas and were quite diverse. There were no restrictions set on any of the producers. It made the channel quite surprising but it also got us in a lot of trouble with the Woodstock city council, the cops and the district attorney, but that's another story.

S&P: In 1978, after eight years in Maple Tree Farm, the last of the Videofreex left Lanesville, which ended the collective. Why did you take this decision to stop the *Lanesville TV* project and not to live together anymore?

Davidson: In 1973 OPEC imposed an oil embargo in response to America's involvement with Israel's Yom Kippur War. This and other causes began a cycle of inflation, making money worth less and less. This impacted the Videofreex, of course, since most of our income at that time came from NYSCA grants, and was relatively fixed. By 1975, when I left for the city, it was harder to sustain life at Maple Tree Farm for the nine people who lived there.

Parry: Many people considered themselves to be full-time artists and they were going in one direction. Others were trying to figure out what was going on, and I put myself in that kind of realm: how do you make a living of this, how do you sustain it? Those are difficult questions but it also seems worthwhile especially because of the connection we developed with the community. To share and export it was a real challenge. While we were developing a pirate television station, cable TV was coming in with access channels which made it completely legal and completely easy to do it and the challenge was: what are you going to do now?! And there were real active experiments, not even experiments, programs that developed out of that. With cable TV, channels were available to whoever subscribed to cable television. At first there weren't very many people but it became a few hundred thousand, which was a lot by our standards. And there were regulations. Over a certain number of subscribers cable TV production had to offer a certain numbers of channels ... and then people realized they could put stuff on it and of course people who were really eager to do community experimentation and community work came along. But the pornographers came along, and ... basically the whackos took over ... Now, I'm a publisher, local newspaper, I'm still in community media, much like *Lanesville TV*. I did a lot of other things. I produced video programs in various ways, and then I get involved with one of the people who visited Lanesville, a guy who worked with Ant Farm and TVTV, but he was a lawyer and later he became the head of something called the Low Power TV Task Force at the Federal Communication Commission and he was working on making TV stations like *Lanesville TV* legal. And he asked me to write a report about *Lanesville TV*. Strangely enough, in 1980, Low Power TV was adopted by this commission of the Federal Government, the one that regulated all broadcasting access. All the news media were interested in the Low Power TV, I think it was on the front page of the New York Times: "First New Broadcast Service in Twenty Years" and it became legal to do what we did in *Lanesville TV* in a much higher power.

S&P: In his essay, *A Proposal for a New Television Network*,[14] Tom Weinberg detailed how after revolutionizing the production and the TV broadcasting, alternate television communities would have to control distribution. He proposed the creation of a new independent television network. Independent video-makers and producers never had their own control on their distribution, but TVTV can be an example of the fact that some video-makers tried to change the way television was made from the inside, by agreeing to be distributed by the major networks. It is also interesting to point out that some of the Videofreex members, after the Maple Tree Farm period, got involved, at various scales, in some bigger productions.

Skip: I went on to specialize in producing and directing hundreds of TV shows including for PBS and National Geographic TV, for websites like myhero.com, and fundraising videos for nonprofits, mostly educational agencies, but I have continued as an independent filmmaker producing video art, single channel work and multi-channel installations, performance videos like *In Motion* with Michael Moschen, cultural documentaries about events and phenomena like Eskimo sports, a rodeo for elephants, bonobos in a zoo in Florida, and my most well-known show *Pick Up Your Feet: The Double*

14 Tom Weinberg, "A Proposal for a New Television Network," (subm. by The Ad Hoc Committee For a New Network, 1990), https://mediaburn.org/wp-content/uploads/2012/08/a-proposal-for-a-new-television-network.pdf.

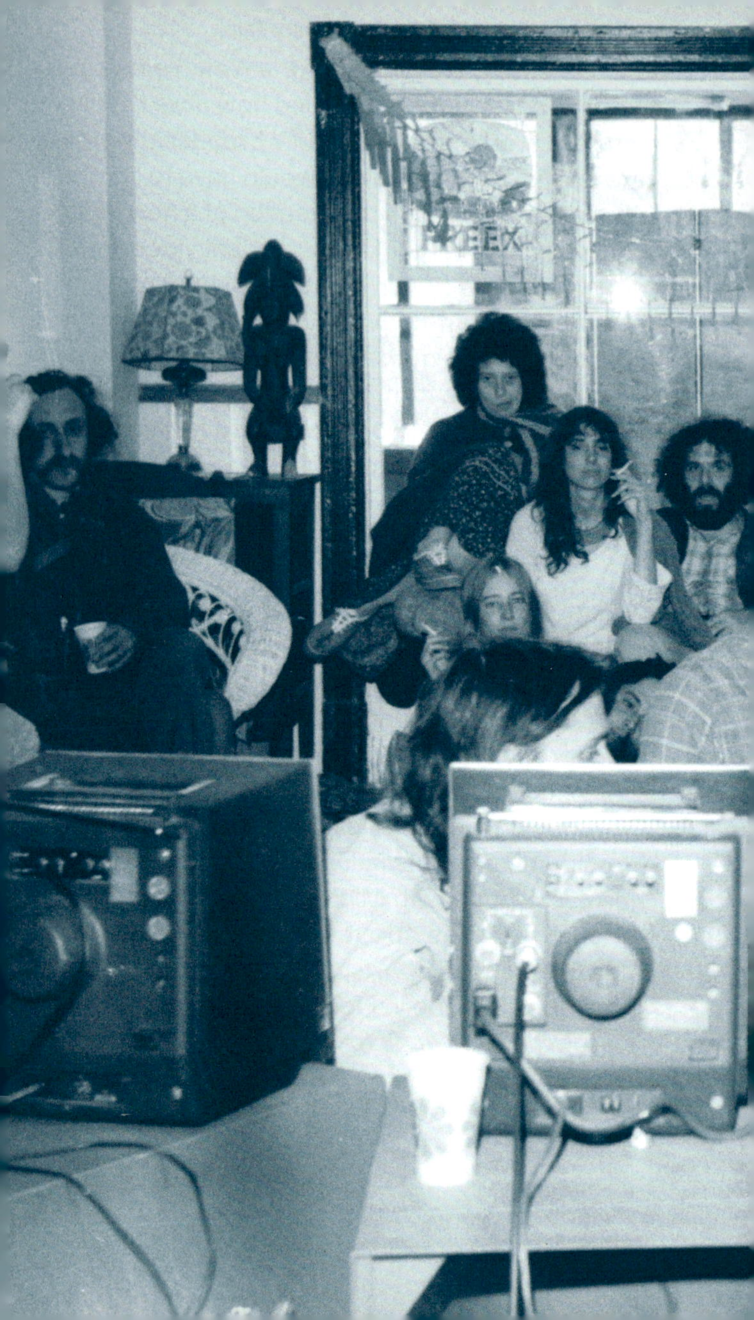

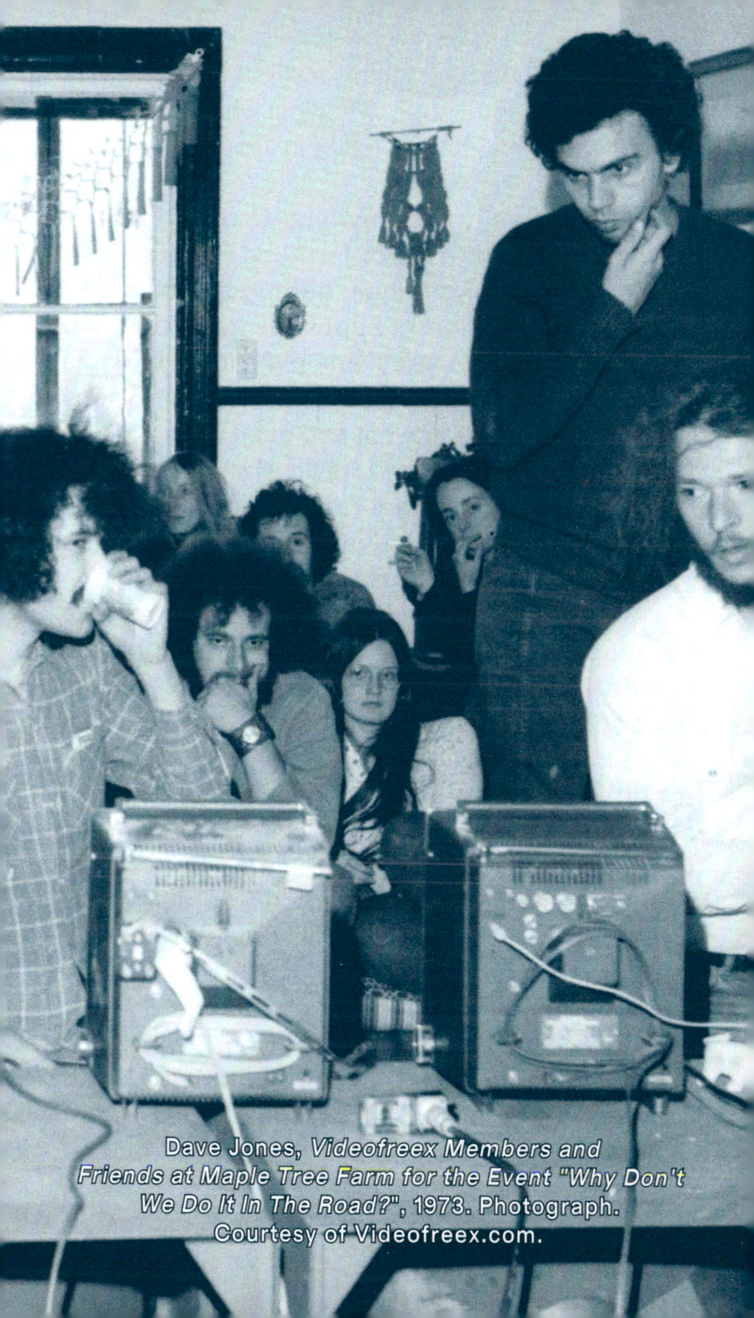

Dave Jones, *Videofreex Members and Friends at Maple Tree Farm for the Event "Why Don't We Do It In The Road?"*, 1973. Photograph. Courtesy of Videofreex.com.

Dutch Show, that I think is still in the collection at Pompidou. I hope to find out while I'm in Paris for the exhibition at Treize in January.

Ann: I never really had anything to do with making videotapes. With Carol, I worked on cataloging things and labelling things, getting some kind of order. I would do sort of supplemental things, like when David went to Israel and did a lot of taping, I would look at the stuff, screen it, and log the tapes in with descriptions of what had been shot. I kind of soaked up from Parry and David what editing was. After I moved back to New York City, my friend Russell Connor called me and said that he had left the museum, to work for the New York State Council on the Arts. He did that for a while and then became an independent producer. He said, "Why don't you come and help me, because I have a show that has to be edited." I was sort of interested in editing because it was like making a collage. I worked for him for three or four years and then I got a job as an editor in an editing house and I spent maybe ten years doing that. I worked for many years on the Barbara Walters' show. I became a nurse in 1992, and finally now can devote my time to my work in mixed media, painting and collage.

Bart: Nancy and I moved twenty miles east into Woodstock, New York, where we incorporated a not-for-profit, public access cable channel that we helped operate for another ten years. It still thrives.

S&P: Videofreex took the decision to digitalize the tapes. What was your relation to the question of conservation and archiving?

Skip: We saved about fifteen hundred tapes, but we recorded thousands. We lost only forty or fifty tapes that were on our shelves in Lanesville, but we lost a lot of tapes by sending originals to other video groups around the world or just recording over previous recordings. Because after we would make a tape, and we might record over it, to recycle and save money. We shoot a tape, we show it on *Friday Night*, and then, we would make another recording on the same tape and show it the next Friday.

Parry: But the issue of preservation is a big question. And maybe as we grow older, the concept of preserving for some of us seems more important, because what else can we do of our lives. That's OK, I think it is fine but I'm not as invested, and I speak only for myself. It doesn't make anything less valuable and I've written about it but that's something I did and I'm doing something else now.

Carol: And the idea of looking for the stuff, finding stuff, was not fun actually. "Did I save this, did I not save this" ... I'd rather not think about it. You know for at least twenty years I never even thought about Videofreex. Maybe thirty. Parry and I, we used to have the tapes in our attic and it pulled the wall away from the ceiling, it was so heavy on the floor. The house was sinking! I had no idea where they were going to go.

Parry: Yes, and Video Data Bank came and took it all away and they catalogued it. The technology that was so wonderful for editing ended up eating much of my tape with blue mold. And I lost several years of work, and I say, you know, maybe I'll find something else to do. Now that I've seen that some of the tapes that have been restored, I'm actually curious.

Davidson: Several of the Videofreex have always been concerned to preserve our tapes. We did not always have the same reasons for wanting to do so, and it took until about 2002 to get a plan together. That was about the same time that Jon Nealon and Jenny Raskin began to approach us.[15] It all came together with Video Data Bank and Jon and Jenny at about the same time.

Abina Manning and Tom Colley: In 2000, Kate Horsfield, a co-founder and then director of the Video Data Bank, met with Parry and Carol and interviewed them as part of Kate and the Video Data Bank's ongoing interview series *On Art and Artists*. From this initial conversation, the process of collaboration on the preservation and distribution of the Freex archive began. It took several years of discussions about the best way ahead for an

15 Jon Nealon and Jenny Raskin directed the documentary *Here Come the Videofreex*, 2016.

agreement to be drawn up between the Videofreex and the Video Data Bank, and for the preservation of the tapes to begin with. In October 2006 an agreement was signed between Video Data Bank's director, Abina Manning, and the Videofreex representative, Skip Blumberg.

> S&P: Videofreex was using the alternate television medium and was supporting—with the *Friday Night* concept, the video theater and *Lanesville TV*—an access to their images as broad as possible. Today, for entirely understandable economic reasons, the diffusion of the tapes are subdued to fees. But what is the impact of this on the diffusion of the work and the political and social aspects of Videofreex work?

Abina & Tom: Founded in the mid-1970s, the Video Data Bank grew out of this same organic and *rhizomatic* time period as the Videofreex. The Video Data Bank has always worked with almost exclusively artistic, activist and countercultural video makers. One tension that we have noticed is that while the work of Video Data Bank and other distributors has been important, and somewhat successful, in both fostering awareness and scholarship of video and media art, it often costs too much for many people to access more work through screening rentals. On the other hand, it is part of our mission to ensure that artists get paid for the exhibition of their work. Video Data Bank TV has been our way to bridge this gap.

S&P: What is the point for you to exhibit Videofreex in the museums and what is the importance of transmitting Videofreex vision and political statement today?

Davidson: The Videofreex moment was unique to its time. The essence of it, the newness of the portable analog video medium, the psychological impact of seeing oneself as an active media participant, not just as a passive viewer, was almost shocking in its intensity. But now these characteristics have largely been subsumed within our constantly changing digital culture. The cell phone is the direct descendent of the Portapak. The Videofreex do have an historic claim. They were present at the beginning of all this, and they were aggressive in pursuing the agenda of change as it applied to all media. They were very early in the process of combining dissemination with dialogue in media. This is important and they are notable for pioneering this. You can argue that museums themselves are elitist institutions, certainly. That was the opinion of some of the Videofreex. But that, in a sense, is to call the entire project of history elitist. There are those who do, who equate history with baggage. I am not one of these.

Skip: At that time we considered that art museums were institutions, were agents of the status quo. They were about preserving what existed. We wanted to forget what existed and just move on. So we saw art museums as agents of the status quo and we were agents of change. And now it is ironic that, suddenly by exposing our politics, the exhibition at the Dorsky,[16] was an agent of change, and the Videofreex are agents of the status quo, and we want our old work preserved and viewed in the hallowed galleries of the art world [*laughs*]. So the context changed. So again yes, as a political act, we are pleased to be reconsidering those years to be years of foment, of social foment, of cultural foment, of artistic foment, and of political foment. There are still wars to protest, and civil rights abuses in the US, meaning unfair limits of minority rights, gender rights, especially women's rights, there are still issues that even though there have been a lot of accomplishments since the 1970s, there is still a ways to go. So yes, we're pleased to become part of the Treize community in Paris, and to interact with it ... to show our work, receive feedback, and find out, especially with the current state of domestic US and world events, if it generates any activism, media activism or political activism, and, since you promised, any parties at Treize.

16 *Videofreex: The Art of Guerilla Television,* the first retrospective exhibition on the work of the Videofreex took place at the Samuel Dorsky Museum of Art in 2015.

Delay of Gratification: A Note on Feedback in Video and Film

Enrico Camporesi

I keep thinking of a detail from a scene in Jean-Luc Godard's *Sauve qui peut (la vie),* (*Every Man for Himself*, 1980). On a classroom blackboard stands the inscription: "*Caïn et Abel Cinéma et Vidéo.*" This witty writing in chalk resembles an equation (it is only missing the equals sign), an operation that seeks to establish a link between two different technologies, with separate histories. As ideal brothers, cinema and video might even be thought of as lookalikes. Siblings, after all, share some visual features, however hidden they might be. But, as the biblical brothers, they necessarily carry within them a conflict.[1] I do not know exactly which of the two is supposed to be the righteous or evil one, but the operation, in its simplicity, hints at a logical progression. Why are they similar? The two of them share an urge to record processes, to restitute movement, to shape time.

Cain and Abel: all generalizations aside, the conflict is right under my eyes. I happen to work in an institution in which video and film have been duly kept apart since the inception of its collections. In 1992 the works previously gathered (since the mid-

1 According to J. Hoberman's reading of Godard's aphorism, though, "the movie-video polarity is pretty much a red herring"—the real polarity being "cinema-television." See J. Hoberman, "Veni, Vidi, Video ...," *Film Comment*, 18, no. 3 (May–June 1982): 34.

1970s) at the Centre Pompidou under the collective name "documentation" were distributed into three separate branches: photography, film, and video. The latter would quickly become "New Media," with the adjective "new" being used to symbolize the breakaway from the "old" photo-filmic paradigm.

Whatever brought about this situation, along with internal affairs of cultural politics, cannot be severed from the discursive space of video art as it was fashioned in the years of its major expansion. Still, to this day, it is reported that a prominent curator would abide by the most naive of definitions to set video and film against one another. "Film mainly looked at itself, whereas video had from the start welcomed the outside world." This quote, approximate and unattributed for matters of decency, shows a twofold bias. The first part gestures at a very specific moment in the history of experimental film, loosely coinciding with the production known as "structural film." Under this much-debated name, one would find a group of filmmakers who "turned upon the form and substance of film and its immediate contexts to define the range of their working materials."[2] More crucially, the latter part of the curator's sentence casts an ideal aura of transparency onto a technology that had, on the contrary, encountered mirror-like reflexivity from its very beginnings. I cannot dwell upon the anecdote of the curator, who

2 Tony Conrad, "Artistic Extensions of the Filmic Image," in *Writings*, eds. Constance DeJong and Andrew Lampert (New York: Primary Information, 2019), 131. Conrad's text was first delivered as a lecture at the Carpenter Center for the Visual Arts, Harvard University (Cambridge, MA) on February 28, 1974.

should just have known better, having been involved in the honorable task of disseminating video art in the museum since its opening in 1977. It is poignant, though, that even a nonchalant, unsubstantiated remark such as the one reported would still bear the traces of the two discourses on video art that David Antin had summed up in the mid-1970s. He identified them under the names "cyberscat" and "formalist rap," the first being "a kind of enthusiastic welcoming prose peppered with fragments of communication theory and McLuhanesque media talk; the other, a rather nervous attempt to locate the 'unique properties of the medium.'"[3]

In 1975, when Antin was writing these lines, video art's trajectory was roughly at the end of its first decade. By 1980, when Godard's *Every Man for Himself* came out, the debate on video art had already entered a new era; its aura of novelty had turned into a renewed theoretical phase. Video, as Antin noted, dismissed its clothes of technological wonder to become an *issue*. The question about its ontology proceeded in the first place from an attempt to scrutinize meticulously the possible differences and affinities between film and video.

It is unlikely that Godard was aware of the whole debate going on around video in the United States, but nonetheless he captured, through the biblical pun, the enraged conflict that was setting one technology against another. At the time Godard did not know about the American experimental filmmaker

3 David Antin, "Television: Video's Frightful Parent," *Artforum* 14, no. 4 (December 1975): 36.

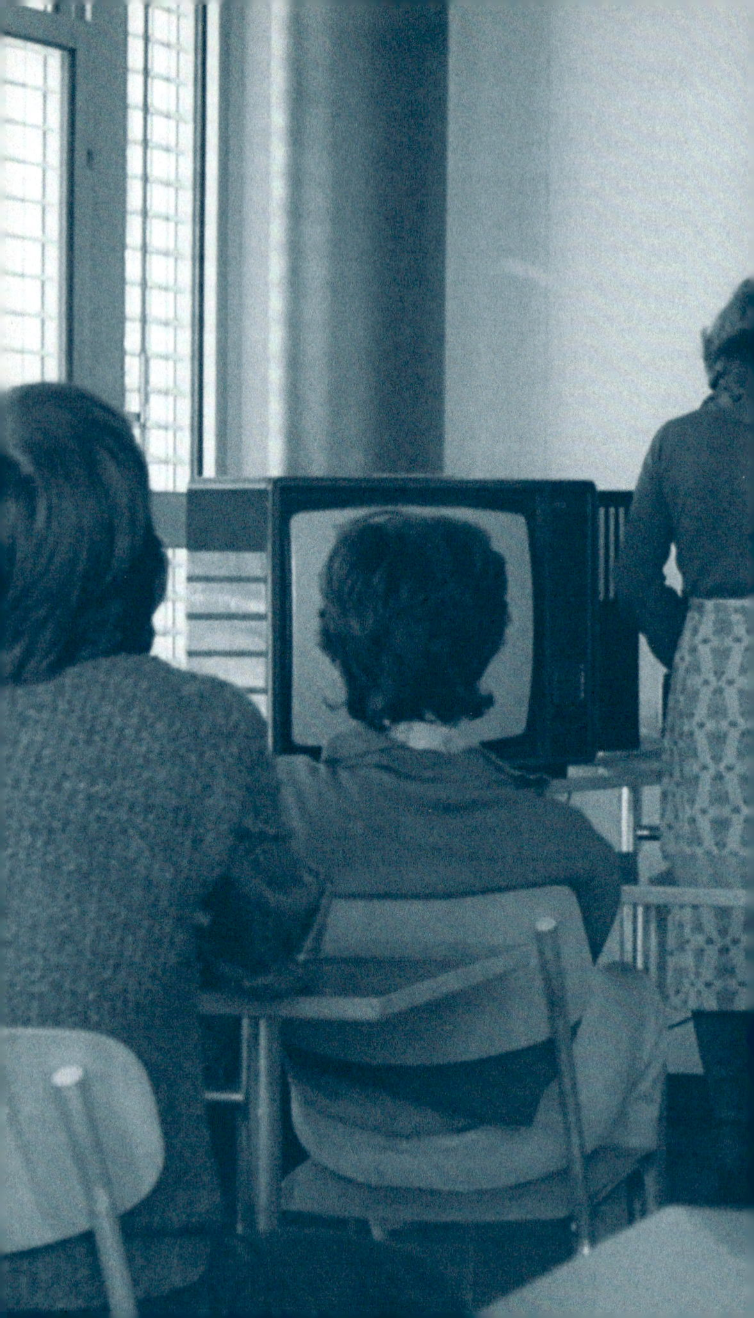

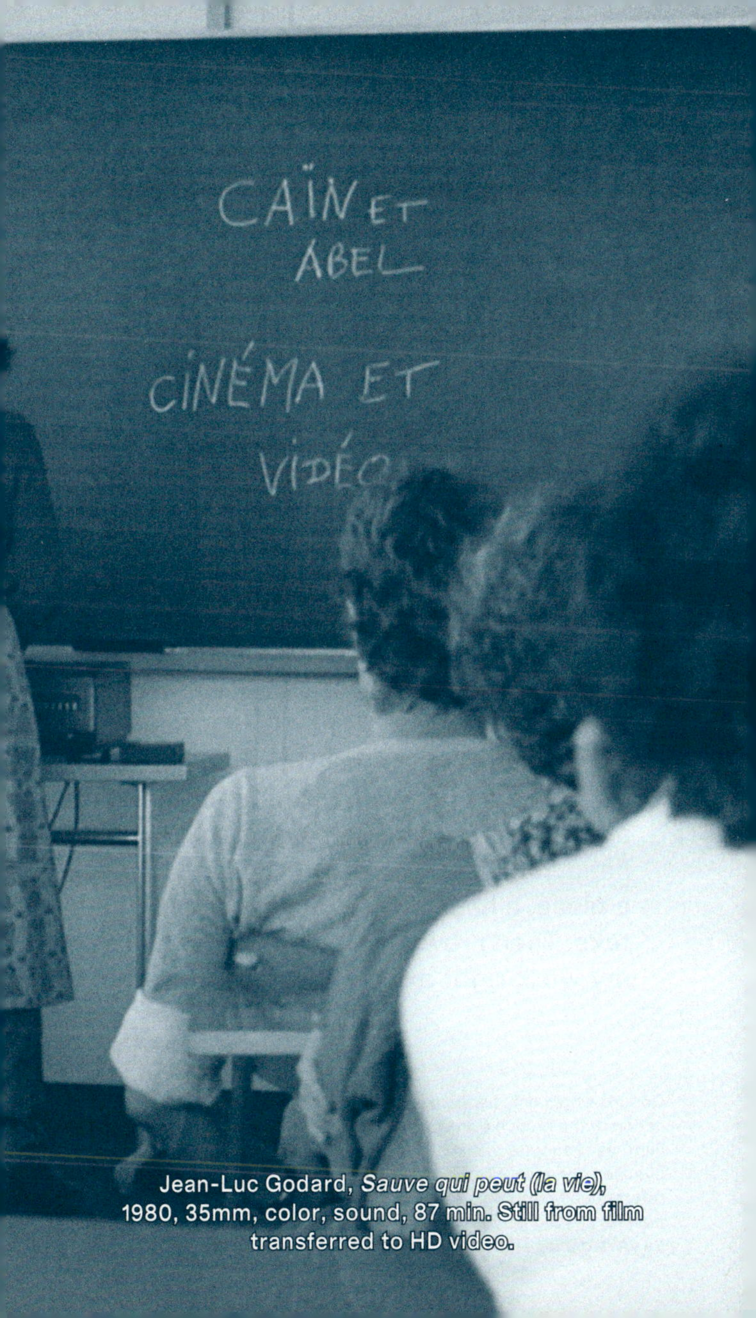

Jean-Luc Godard, *Sauve qui peut (la vie)*,
1980, 35mm, color, sound, 87 min. Still from film
transferred to HD video.

and photographer Hollis Frampton,[4] whose conference "On the Future of the Television" was published in the December 1974 issue of *Artforum*. Frampton's observations attempted to analyze how seemingly similar video and film would appear and how distant, in fact, they are. Among the tools and references summoned to understand the issue at stake, what strikes me is the psychoanalytical frame retrieved in order to read the image production process.

> Sigmund Freud, in *Civilization and Its Discontents*, suggests that civilization depends upon the delay of gratification. I might caricature this to mean that, by denying myself one hundred million lollipops, I'll end up with a steam yacht ... and go on to envision a perfect civilization entirely devoid of gratification. But every filmmaker must perforce believe in part of this cartoon, since filmmaking involves long delays, during which the work more than once disappears into the dark night of the mind and the laboratory. I remember, on the other hand, the first time I ever used video. I made a piece, a half-hour long, in one continuous take. Then I rewound the notation, and saw my work right away. That was three years

4 Godard would only become aware of Frampton thanks to the publication of the French translation of his 1971 text "For a Metahistory of Film" as "Pour une métahistoire du film: notes et hypothèses à partir d'un lieu commun," *Trafic 21* (Spring 1997). Subsequently he explicitly referenced Frampton's essay in the final section of *Histoire(s) du cinéma (4B: Les Signes parmi nous,* 1998) and in his most recent feature, *Le Livre d'image* (2018).

> ago, and to tell the truth some part of my puritanical filmmaker's nature remains appalled to this day. The gratification was so intense and immediate that I felt confused.[5]

The temporal hiatus in shooting, developing, and printing filmic material can be interpreted as the delay that tends to be cherished in the mature stages of the appreciation of pleasure. The distance between the process of the production of images and its result, in a canonical chain of photo-filmic operations bears, for Frampton, a resemblance to the delayed mechanics of the libido. The euphoria triggered by the suppression of such delay in video then seems to reconnect, in Frampton's text, with a childish jubilation.

Collapsing image recording and its on-screen restitution is a recurrent trope in the literature on video art. The phenomenon, mostly cited under the label of "feedback," stands also at the center of Rosalind Krauss's 1976 essay "Video: The Aesthetics of Narcissism." Video, in Krauss's reading, articulates this characteristic in two distinct ways: in works on tape it places the body of the performer at its center, whereas in installations it displays the body of the viewer. In both cases, the distinctive trait is the "simultaneous reception and projection of an image."[6]

5 Hollis Frampton, "The Withering Away of the State of Art," *Artforum* 13, no. 4 (December 1974): 54. The text was first delivered at the conference "Open Circuits: The Future of Television," Museum of Modern Art, New York, January 23–25, 1974.

6 Rosalind Krauss, "Video: The Aesthetics of Narcissism," *October* 1 (Spring 1976): 52.

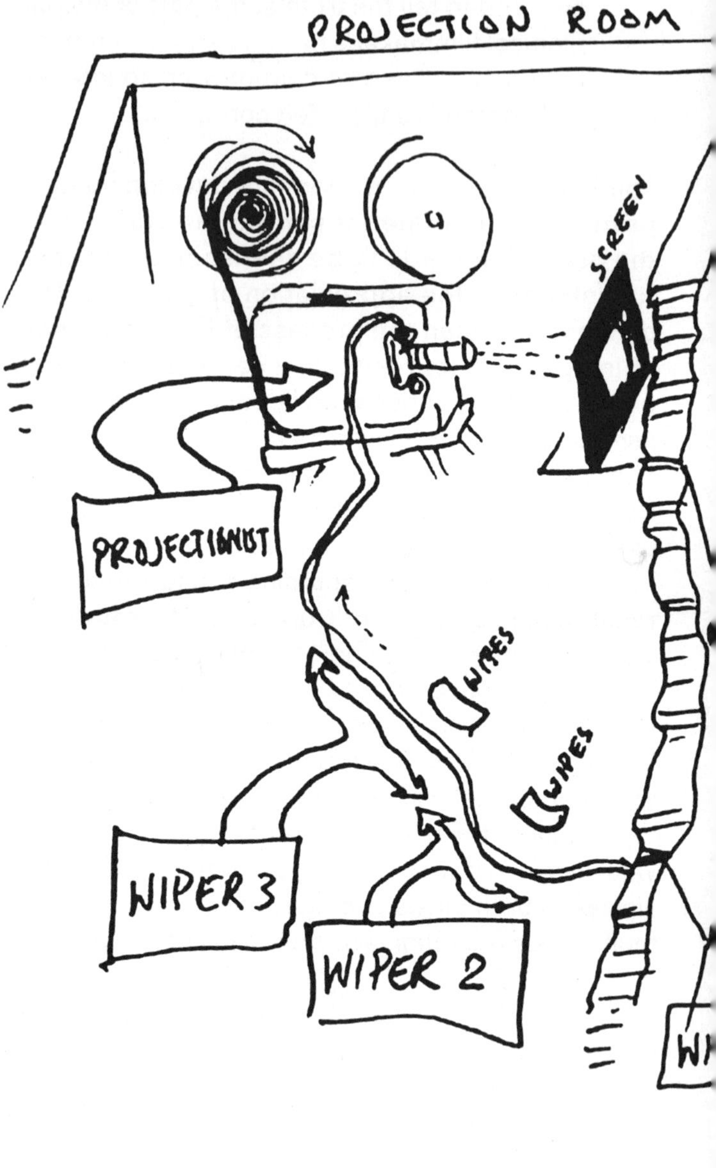
PROJECTION ROOM
SCREEN
PROJECTIONIST
WIPES
WIPES
WIPER 3
WIPER 2

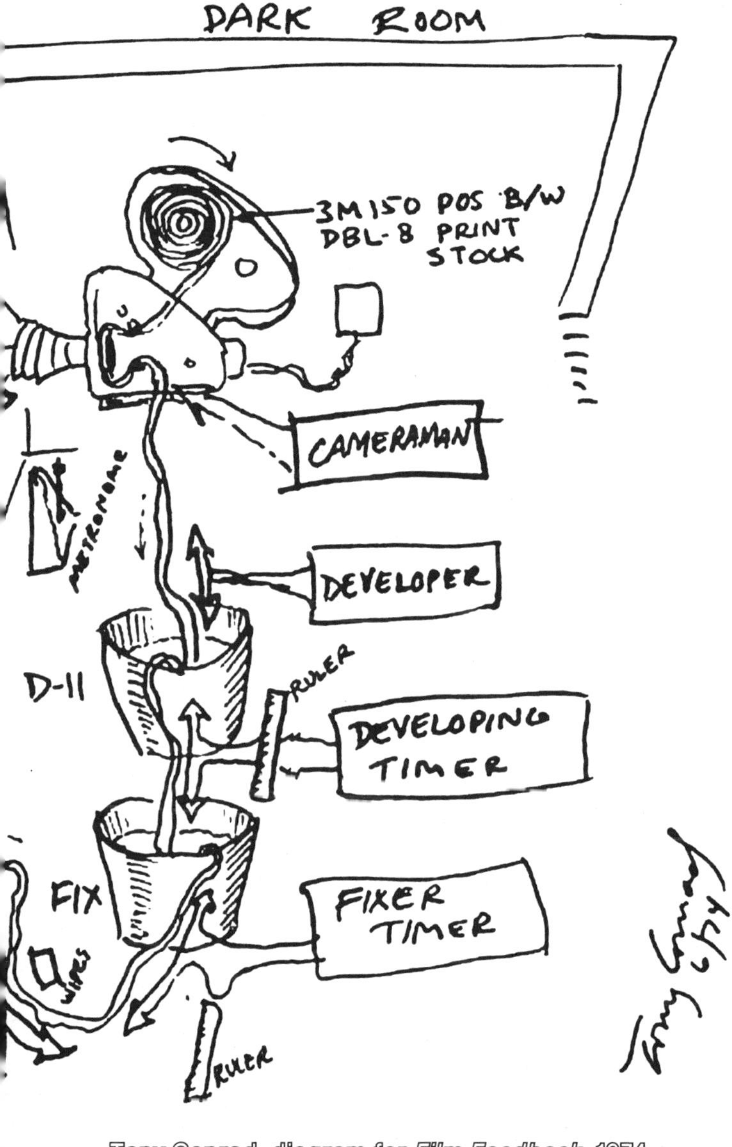

Tony Conrad, diagram for *Film Feedback*, 1974.

To use Frampton's words: video suppresses the filmic delay of gratification.

Despite her likely cognizance of the publication of Frampton's conference text in *Artforum*, Krauss does not cite him directly. And yet she seems to elaborate an interpretative frame that owes something to the quick Freudian reference injected into his considerations. But Krauss goes one step further. While the recollection of a Freudian quote is evidently tongue-in-cheek for Frampton, Krauss is committed to analyzing video through a much more rigorous Lacanian reading of narcissism. In doing so, she substitutes the fast forward, openly whimsical, understanding of the delay of gratification in a social frame with another interpretative apparatus, that of a "psychological situation, the very terms of which are to withdraw attention from an external object [...] and invest it in the Self."[7] In short, the whole architecture of her essay points at demonstrating that "the medium of video is narcissism."[8]

Whether via *Civilization and Its Discontents* or *A General Introduction to Psychoanalysis*, both Frampton and Krauss succeed in locating the ontology of video in the possibility of immediacy, that is: the literal erasure of a delay between recording and seeing. Practitioners would nod, by pushing the process to the verge of abstraction, excluding the presence of the artist (and in some cases, one might argue, that of the viewer). As video art pioneer Woody Vasulka put it, video feedback, the "dynamic

7 Krauss, "Video," 57.
8 Krauss, "Video," 50.

flow of imagery created by the camera looking at its own monitor [...] was often (and still is) the first phenomenon that seduced users of video by its sheer beauty."[9] What else but aesthetic sublimation could come to rescue video-making from the subtle hints of either a childish behavior or psychosis?[10]

The "sheer beauty" of video feedback is the result of a non-mediated confrontation between parts of the same technological apparatus. This possibility is, ultimately, its distinctive quality, or even its foundational ontology. Going against the grain, in 1974, Tony Conrad produced a counter intuitive response to the supposedly stable grounds of video essentialism. Being fed up with the very notion of "medium specificity," the artist conceived and staged, during the course of a class at Antioch College, "one of the few instances in which the film has ever been worked with in such a manner as to make the image visible before the roll of film has been completely shot."[11] The process of what would

9 Woody Vasulka, "Video Feedback with Audio Input Modulation and CVI Data Camera," in *Eigenwelt der Apparate-Welt: Pioneers of Electronic Art*, eds. David Dunn, Woody Vasulka, and Steina Vasulka (Linz: Ars Electronica, 1992), 148. Quoted in Yvonne Spielmann, "Video: From Technology to Medium," *Art Journal* 65, no. 3 (Fall 2006): 61.

10 On psychosis and narcissism, Jacques Laplanche and Jean-Bertrand Pontalis recall that "it was the study of the psychoses, in particular, which led Freud to the recognition that the subject can take his own self as a love-object". See "Ego-Libido/Object-Libido," *The Language of Psycho-Analysis*, trans. Donald Nicholson-Smith (London: Karnac Books, 1988), 150, orig. pub. *Vocabulaire de la psychanalyse* (Paris: Presses universitaires de France, 1967).

11 Tony Conrad, lecture at the Carnegie Museum of Art (Pittsburgh, PA), November 13, 1974. The lecture, part of the Independent Film Makers Series organized by Sally Dixon, was recorded onto half-inch videocassette and is now digitized and accessible online on the institution's website (access no. fv001/002/160/A), https://records.cmoa.org/things/60df673c-677a-

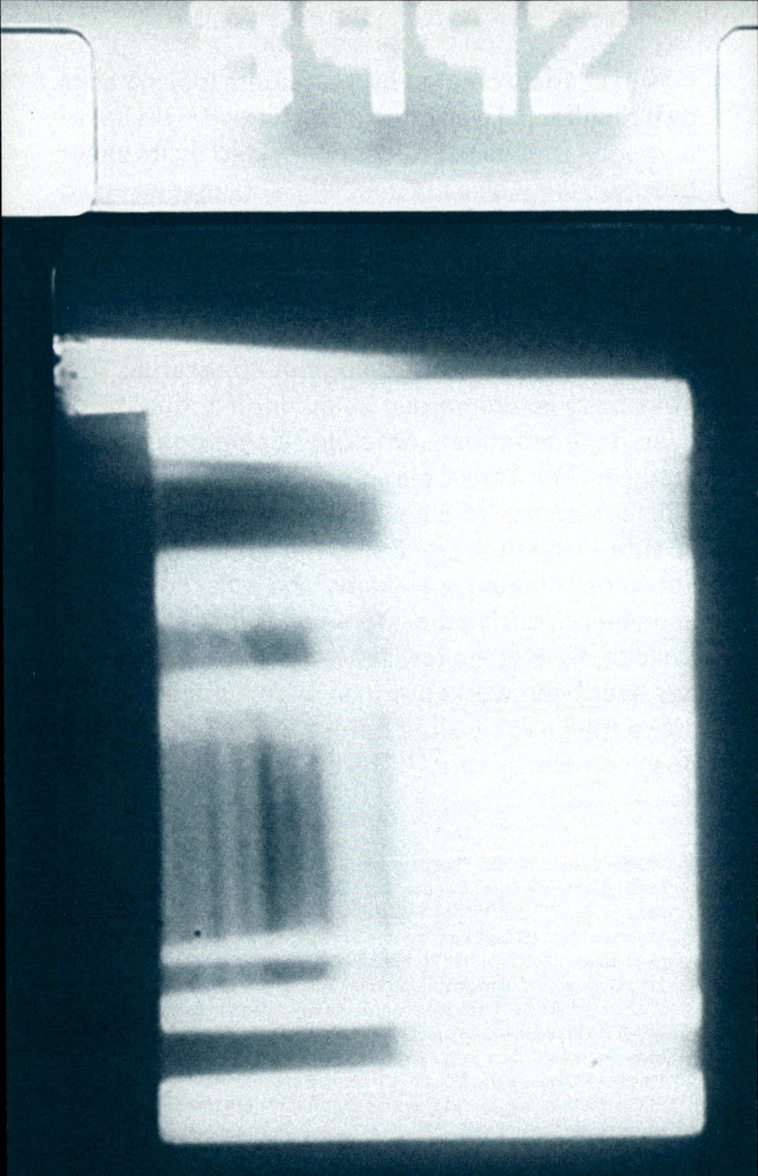

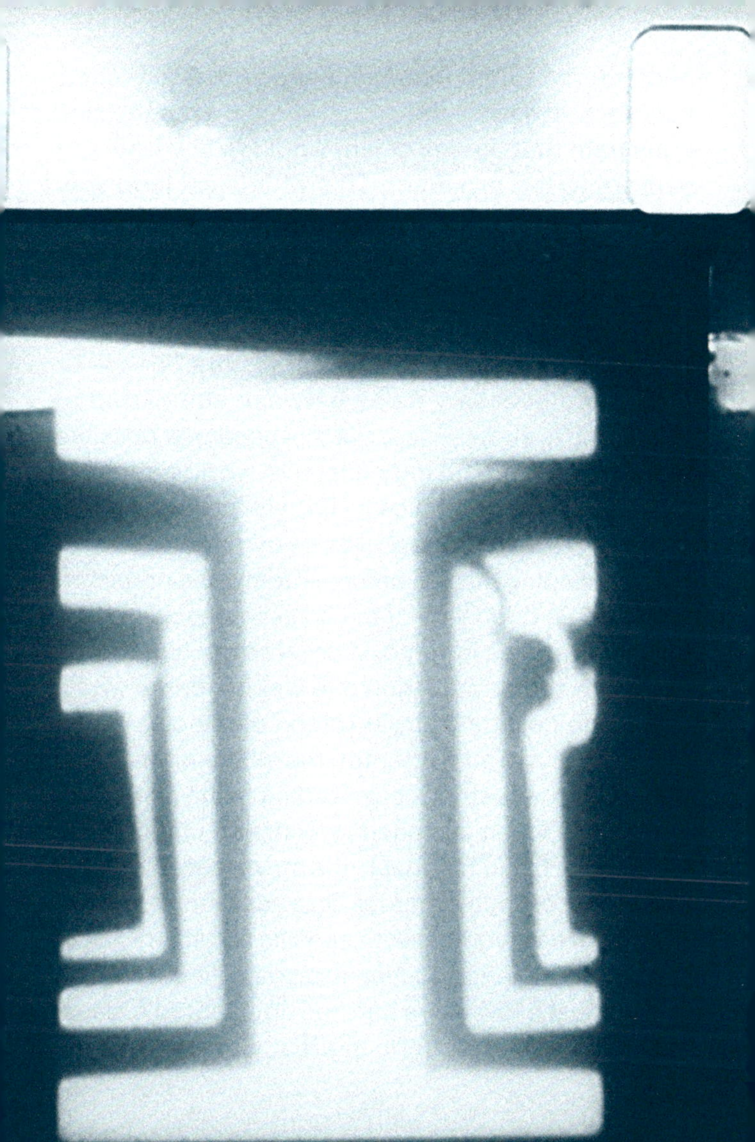

Tony Conrad, *Film Feedback*, 1974,
16mm film, black and white, silent, 14 min.
Stills from film. © Anthology Film Archives.

become the 16mm film *Film Feedback* is sketched out in a drawing by the artist, which traces the sinuous path that the roll of film would follow from the camera to the projector. This whimsical loop was a deliberate counter-attack on the foundational narrative of video. As he mentioned recalling this experience later: "Instantaneous image feedback was then seen as video's 'essence,' but this was film team-developed and reshot in real time."[12]

The necessary delay between shooting and projecting is suppressed, but this becomes possible thanks to a painstaking collective work: gathering eight people to rhythmically dip, with precise timing, film into the developer, and three other people scrupulously wiping the film before entering the projector. This is the hidden side of the achievement. Contrary to what happens in video, in order to get film to look at itself without mediation one would need a whole crew. The collective organization of the classroom mimics, in Conrad's attempt, the whole operational (most often industrial) chain leading to the final product of film. Albeit excluded in Conrad's ultimate depiction of a filmic feedback, the movie set stands out as another collective model. On a set, labor is distributed between workers with specific skills. To each of the workers the production assigns a different task. In 1970, just a few years before Tony Conrad's classroom project, an American artist with an in-depth

4ff7-8237-79cd3c1941f2. I wish to thank Andrew Lampert for directing me to this important resource.

12 Tony Conrad, "Media Study: Tony Conrad," in *Writings*, 288, orig. pub in *Artforum* 51, no. 1 (September 2012): 419.

knowledge of movie production had conceived another strategy for film to look at itself. Based in Los Angeles, Morgan Fisher attended film school at USC and UCLA, and therefore had been trained to integrate the hierarchical organization of a classical movie set. However, his 11-minute film *Production Stills* bears little resemblance to any ordinary production of the kind he was supposed to work on. What does the film show? Consisting of a single shot, the frame opens onto a white surface; a hand sticks four drawing pins into the edges of an ideal rectangle. Among the background noises and fragments of conversations, we overhear a camera clicking. A Polaroid picture is then displayed within the frame. The image shows nothing else but a portion of the set, the very same environment in which the 16mm film we are watching is produced. The operation is repeated seven more times (eight shots being the standard in the Polaroid camera pack), thus revealing the whole crew and the machines on stage, until the end of the roll of film. As Fisher himself recalls, *Production Stills*

> enacts the model of Hollywood production: a Mitchell camera on a Moviola crab dolly on a sound stage, a Fisher sound boom for the microphone, and, in a condensed form, a Hollywood crew, including a still photographer.[13]

13 Morgan Fisher, "*Production Stills*," in *Morgan Fisher: Writings*, eds. Sabine Folie and Susanne Titz (Cologne: Walther König, 2012), 30. Fisher's notes on *Production Stills* are the revised version of a text originally published in 1985 as a program note for a screening at the Collective for

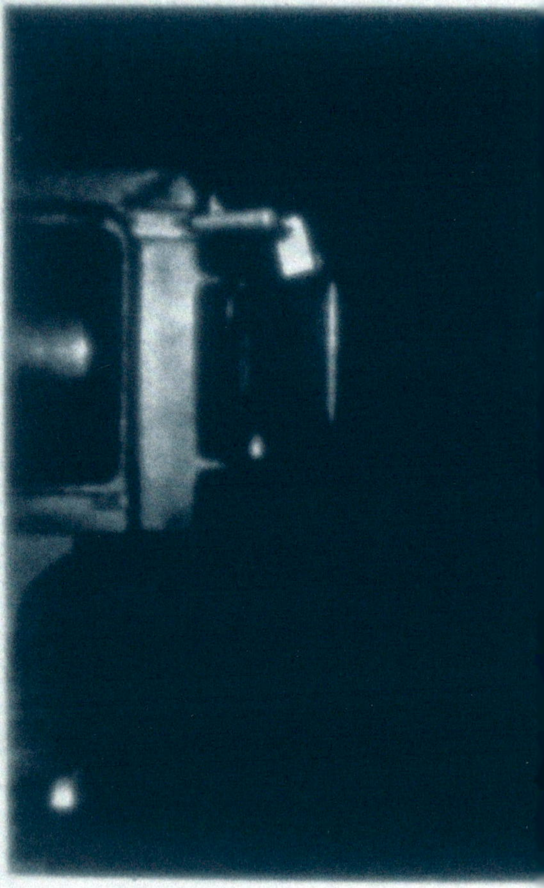

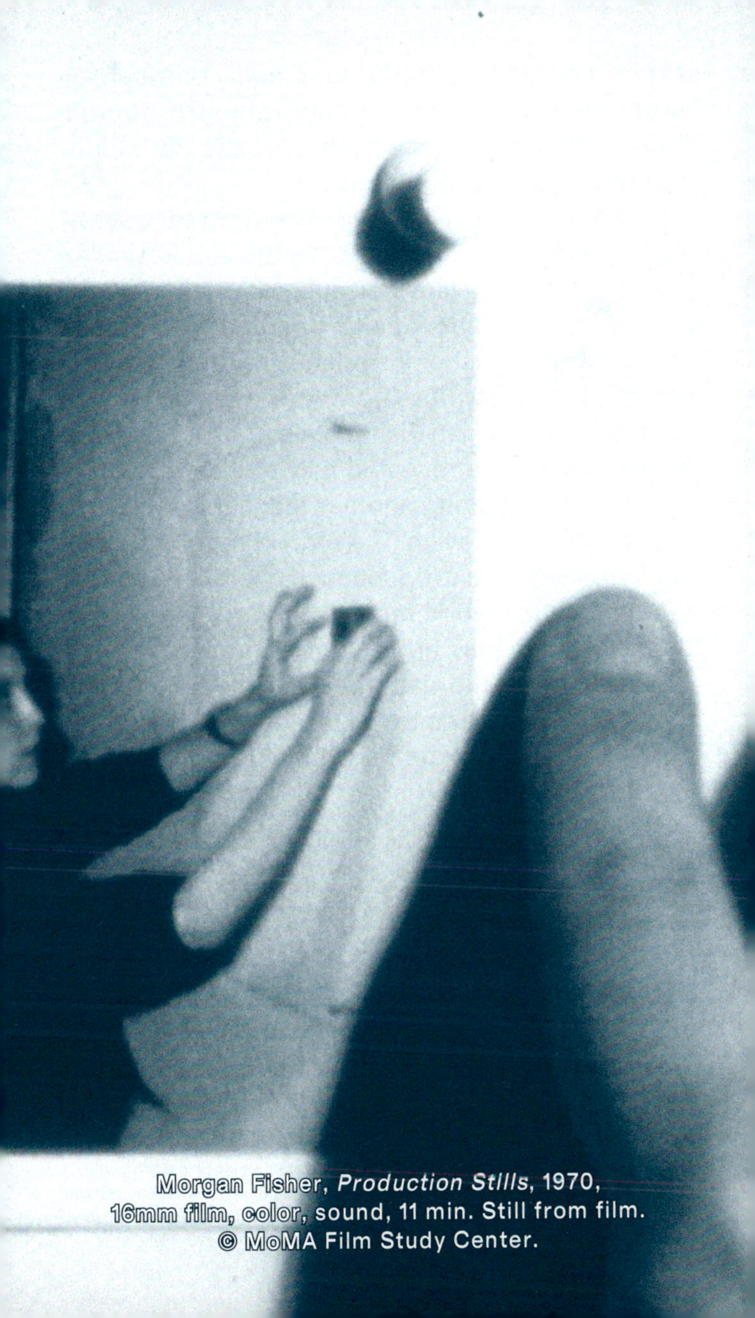

Morgan Fisher, *Production Stills*, 1970,
16mm film, color, sound, 11 min. Still from film.

It is ironic that this important display of means is aimed at a self-reflexive operation: *Production Stills* is "a movie that simply records this documentation of its production."[14]

For Morgan Fisher and Tony Conrad, operating in the first half of the 1970s, the aim is similar: they seek to make film look at itself. But while Conrad and his students design and operate within a closed system, Fisher introduces a supplementary axiom of visibility. As Thom Andersen noticed in his essay on Morgan Fisher's films, "the cinematic apparatus can be revealed fully and scrupulously only by incorporating another mechanical recording system into the film."[15] A form of temporal delay accompanies the introduction of another recording system into the work, but it is this very same delay that allows the full depiction of labor on set.

Ultimately, the hiatus between the process and the final result brings to the foreground something that video feedback tends to hide from the viewer. Contrary to the solitary act of video, configuring film to look at itself is a collective endeavor.[16] In moving image-making, then, labor might be the actual "delay of gratification." Being immediate, the video feedback

Living Cinema, New York, and subsequently published in *Fate of Alien Modes*, ed. Constanze Ruhm (Vienna: Secession, 2003).

14 Thom Andersen, "Pebbles Left on the Beach: The Films of Morgan Fisher," in *Morgan Fisher: Two Exhibitions*, eds. Sabine Folie and Susanne Titz (Cologne: Walther König, 2012), 201, also pub. in *Cinema Scope* 38 (Spring 2009): 37–43.

15 Thom Andersen, "Pebbles Left on the Beach," 202.

16 This does not mean that a collective organization of labor is definitively excluded in video practice. See on this point Ina Blom, "Inside Equipment (Studio Practice)," in *The Autobiography of Video: The Life and Times of a Memory Technology* (Berlin: Sternberg Press, 2016), 127–157.

portrays itself as foundational. It asserts a natural law of technology. As a constructed phenomenon, instead, film feedback unveils a critical impulse. Both apparatuses though, in their self-reflexive configuration, might tend towards a pleasurable outcome.

Locating in the "delay of gratification" the main difference between film and video projects libido onto the intellectual backdrop of the discussion. Hollis Frampton pointed it out while summing-up his 1974 lecture via a recollection of *Civilization and its Discontents*. And it is to a footnote included in the second chapter of the same book that I, in turn, have to take inspiration from. While touching upon the relationship between work and pleasure, Freud had to admit: "it is not possible, within the limits of a short survey, to discuss adequately the significance of work for the economics of the libido."[17] As frustrating as it might sound, this would be a matter for further investigation.

17 Sigmund Freud, *Civilization and Its Discontents*, ed. and trans. James Strachey (New York: W.W. Norton & Company, 1961), 27, orig. pub. *as Das Unbehagen in der Kultur* (Vienna: Internationaler Psychoanalytischer Verlag, 1930).

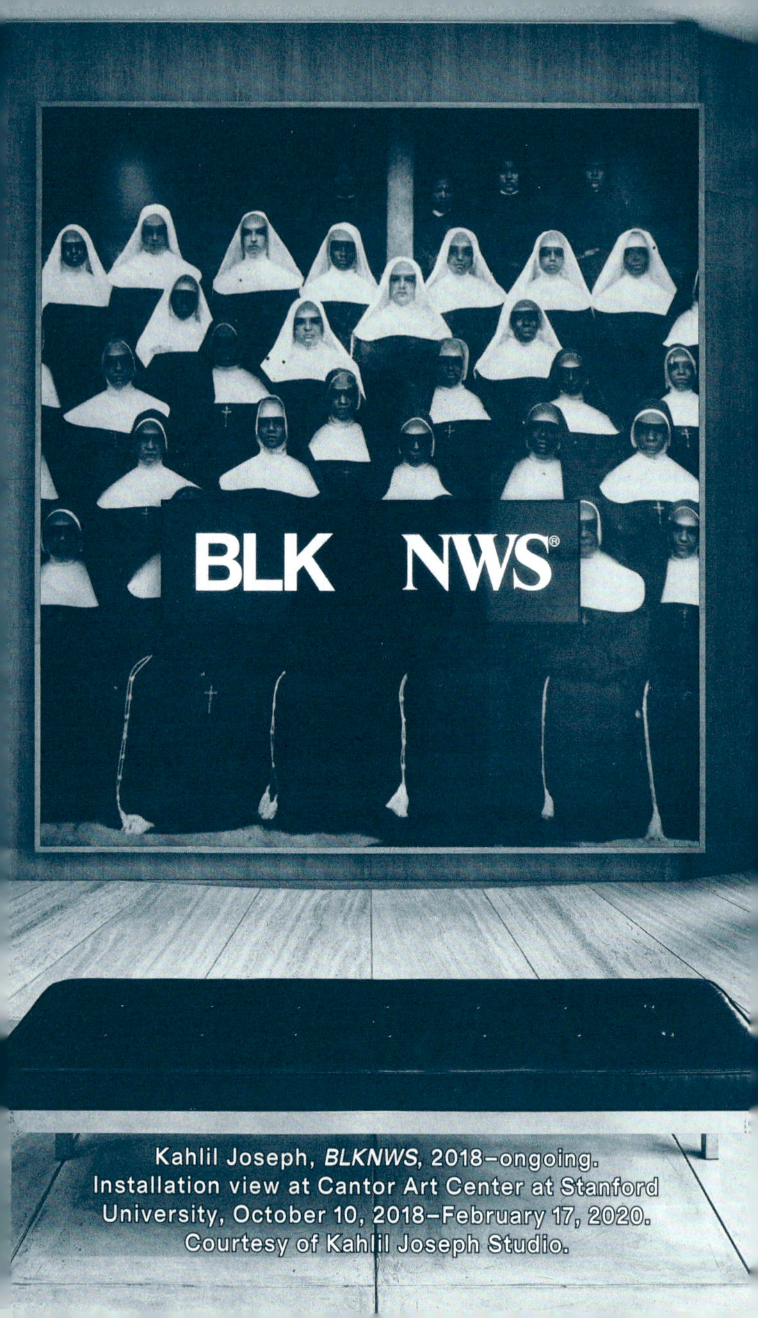

Kahlil Joseph, *BLKNWS*, 2018–ongoing.
Installation view at Cantor Art Center at Stanford University, October 10, 2018–February 17, 2020.
Courtesy of Kahlil Joseph Studio.

BLKNWS and Response-Ability: Who Is Speaking, Where, and How?

Vera Dika

> I like how I felt connected to the video, as well as being sad for how unfair the world is today, acting like we all don't bleed the same.
> Alieser Ferrer, Student
> New Jersey City University

BLKNWS by Kahlil Joseph is a multichannel video installation presented at the 2019 Art Biennale in Venice that employs systems of opposition. Greeted with great acclaim at Biennale, *BLKNWS* offers news from a black perspective, showing black life as vibrant, compassionate, funny, and beautiful, and does so in a way that dominant white audiences rarely see. And while this shift in ideological content may seem like a way to counter the control of the white mass media, if only on a symbolic level, Joseph also engages the exhibition and distribution of *BLKNWS* to critical effect. First to note is that in the showing of *BLKNWS* at the Biennale, Joseph raises a double awareness. In one sense he underlines the impossibility of responding in mutual exchange with the mass media, or with what Jean Baudrillard had termed "irresponsibility," literally, that characteristic of the media that actively prevents the viewer's response.[1] After all, what is shown in Venice is a closed-circuit TV feed with alternative content, not network news. On the other hand, Joseph makes a crucial displacement. By allowing us to view the news from a black subject position at the Biennale, Joseph permits a new visibility to emerge, that is: the visibility of an *absence* from within the art institution itself. We become aware of that the exchange is not a mutual one. *BLKNWS* is once again speaking to a predominantly white privileged audience and doing so in the significant absence of a black American community. Political, social, and economic realities become apparent by this displacement, as well as our complicity. And while it could be noted that all art that comes from other countries and communities at the Biennale are impacted by a similar type of displacement, in Joseph's work, this positioning is further used as a point of opposition and of articulation.

A black American community, and importantly, the black diaspora that is the subject of *BLKNWS*, is largely absent from the viewing audience in Venice, and so highlights the basis of a non-exchange within the art world as well. This is made explicit by Joseph who has designed the background wall around the dual panel video screens on which *BLKNWS* is broadcast.

Here we see a floor to ceiling photograph of a seated group of black nuns who stare out at the pre-

1 Jean Baudrillard, "Requiem for the Media," in For a *Critique of the Political Economy of the Sign*, trans. Charles Levin (St. Louis: Telos Press, 1981), 164–184, orig. pub. *Pour une critique de l'economie politique du signe*, (Paris: Éditions Gallimard, 1972).

dominately white audience now seated in the Giardini (*BLKNWS* is also mounted in the Arsenale where a background image features a group similarly seated black soldiers) and we stare back.[2] We, those who have comfortably traveled to Venice, are thereby confronted with a racial, ethnic, and economic divide.

BLKNWS accosts the viewer with an awareness of the dominant white ideology at work, not only in the news, but in other white institutions, of which the Biennale is a part. Here we see Joseph's implementation of the principal of a dialectical montage, an operating strategy that characterizes much of *BLKNWS* in its organization of space and time, as well as in its manipulation of content. As famously described by Sergei Eisenstein, dialectical montage employs an oppositional clash between cinematic elements, a clash that results in the rise of a third term and stimulates critical thinking.[3] The video *BLKNWS* is composed of music, dialogue, images, and sounds taken largely from found footage. These fragments come from movies, for example, TV news (both actual and staged), music videos, sports events, personal footage, etc. all gleaned from a variety of internet sources including YouTube, Twitter, Facebook, In-

2 Joseph has explained that this image is "symbolic of the importance of family, of the importance of visual documentation, of the importance of the gaze, of staring history in the eyes. It is also a reminder of our American superstructure to undermine, erase, ignore and dismantle the black family, black history, black enterprise and, more generally, black assembly." From the brochure of the exhibition *BLKNWS*, Wadsworth Atheneum Museum of Art, also available at https://www.thewadsworth.org/wp-content/uploads/2019/11/WA-MATRIX-183-Brochure-6-pages.pdf.

3 Sergei Eisenstein, "A Dialectical Approach to Film Form," in *Film Form: Essays in Film Theory*, trans. Jay Leyda (New York: Harcourt, 1969), 61–62. First publ. 1949.

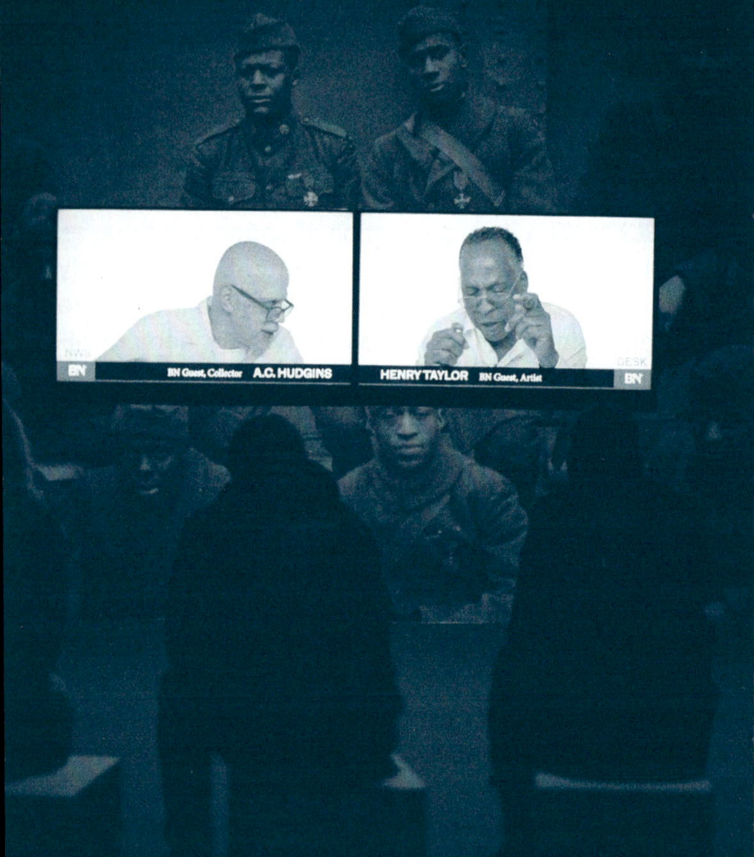

Kahlil Joseph, *BLKNWS*, 2018–ongoing.
Installation view at 58th International Art Exhibition (Arsenale), Venice 2019. Photo by Luke Lynch.
Courtesy of Kahlil Joseph Studio.

stagram, or Joseph says, "I use anything I can put into a computer."[4] Brought to us by a two panel presentation, each screen compares and contrasts its content by linking shots according to oppositional and compatible movement, sound, and mood.

In so doing, Joseph employs the concept of dialectical montage as an operating principle on several levels: in the viewing space, in editing, and then also in the exhibition and the distribution of his work. *BLKNWS* is on view at the Biennale and in other significant venues. It can be seen, for example, at Stanford University, where the installation was originally incubated; or at the Underground Museum, a venue located in a Black and Latino working-class neighborhood of Los Angeles (for the specific purpose of bringing an art museum "within walking distance" of the people) and founded by Joseph's late brother Noah Davis and his wife Karon; or as a twenty-minute video excerpt at New Jersey City University (NJCU) where it was shown as part of my avant-garde film class. Joseph kindly sent us the episode of his work after I made a call to the Underground Museum and requested it. The screening of *BLKNWS* at NJCU will be the subject of the remainder of my essay.

Joseph's intention across all these displacements (a strategy that initially included an attempt to broadcast an ongoing *BLKNWS* program on mainstream TV, but the offer was declined) is to present a counter-narrative to the mass media. But it is also

4 Emily Rose, email to author regarding an unpublished essay by Helen Molesworth, August 6, 2019.

an attempt to complete the conditions of a media message as an *exchange* between speaker and listener. Joseph's goal is to open the work, to cause a rupture, and so allow a response, a responsibility.

In 1974 Baudrillard had called for transgressive gestures to counter the mass media, to "smash the code," as he states. To this end, Baudrillard found that the graffiti scrawled on the walls on city streets during the events of May '68 in France countered the hegemony of the media in terms of the people's ability to respond. He writes:

> Graffiti is transgressive [...] because it responds *there*, on the spot, and breaks the fundamental role of non-response enunciated by the media [...] It doesn't lend itself to deciphering as a text rivaling commercial discourse, it presents itself as a transgression.[5]

And while it could be argued that today, with our collective access to the internet, we can post our opinions regarding the media any time we want, we are still not on the level of an exchange, moreover, we are detached from a material space and a physical community. Joseph manipulates form and content in *BLKNWS*, presenting found footage in an enervating series of oppositional clashes between sound, image, and meaning. But in finding different venues for exhibition he goes farther, confronting the viewer spatially and contextually

5 Baudrillard, *For a Critique of the Political Economy of the Sign*, 183–184.

in various educational, art, and regional locations, encouraging channels of communication to open from within the viewing community itself.

The goal of Joseph's work is to allow a response from his intended audience, a response of the audience to the speaker of the message, as an exchange, and within a lived community of viewers. And even if the community is a small, or marginal, this has important symbolic implications, and this is part of the integral structure of *BLKNWS* itself. First to note is that *BLKNWS* itself is not a closed or completed work, but always in the process of being made. With updates and new and material added to the existing work, *BLKNWS* it is not edited by Joseph alone, but by an editorial team comprised of young, diverse individuals.

The project of this team is to always be in the process of discussion with each other, challenging the dominant media with their ideas, and continuously reformulating the piece. In relationship to the wider scope of the media, this is a relatively small gesture, yet it defines of the existence of a community. It says, "we are here." So too, the episode from *BLKNWS* that was submitted to the community of NJCU students initially allowed them to be identified, and ultimately, to speak back, to exchange with the speaker of the work of art. This was encouraged by Joseph who specifically requested to hear what the students had to say about his *BLKNWS*. The students responded by writing him thank you letters, a few of which I have included below. Like the writers of graffiti on the city streets, the response is immediate and of its place and time. The students speak for themselves through their writings, and in so doing, help to "radically checkmate the dominant order"[6] because of the change in the discursive model, as Baudrillard had proposed.

To re-cap, Joseph stages a three-pronged attack, a spatial affront in Venice, for example, to foreground the absence of black bodies by his site-specific work, an oppositional strategy to foster critical thinking, and then as several strategies to encourage voiced or written responses among lived members. I believe this impulse to bring the work to the people is what prompted Joseph to send a link *BLKNWS* to NJCU. This began after I attended the Venice Biennale and was duly impressed by Joseph's work. Returning home, I made a cold call to the Underground Museum and explained that I taught a diverse population of a students at NJCU, many of which were the first in their families to earn a college degree. I also mentioned that I wanted to show the students in my avant-garde film class contemporary work that would inspire their own art making. Joseph commented that he remembered that moment as a student when he realized, in response to a work of art, "I can do that." Joseph sent us the link. Rather than provide my interpretation of *BLKNWS*, I will offer the students' responses. The letters below were chosen because of their insightful comments from a particular cultural perspective. They are from a class composed primarily of black and Latino students, all in their late

6 Baudrillard, For a Critique of the Political Economy of the Sign, 184.

teens or early twenties. My personal reactions, from my white viewing position, will briefly follow.

> Dear Kahlil Joseph,
> Thank you for allowing our class to watch your work. It was very interesting and powerful. I just wanted to say that I loved the two videos simultaneously playing side by side. Especially when the two videos were contradicting each other. It really made me pick and choose what to see and when and how much time I wanted to dedicate my eyes and mind to one piece. I didn't feel like I was "watching" something for my viewing pleasure but rather critically engaging with your piece. I like that all of the media was fairly recent, so your work was something of our time which made it more entertaining to watch as opposed to some old films and news reels. This work really made me think of how scary and cruel the world is. And the future scares me too. It's funny that our professor showed us your work at the time that she did because I too am planning to make an installation with several videos playing at once. I want to show the madness going on not just in the United States, but all around the world. *BLKNWS* really gave me some more insight into creating my piece. So, thank you again for permitting our class to watch this.
>
> Sincerely,
> Ebony Torres

Dear Mr. Joseph,
The exclusive segment of *BLKNWS* shared with New Jersey City University (NJCU) was phenomenal. There were many moments that stood out and brought so much joy, from Maya Angelou on powerful black mothers, to "Unravel the Skin," inferring how Black women have been underappreciated on film. The music too was so amazing, I tried to Shazam before it went off. I even became so impatient for new music from Frank Ocean because his voice is incredible and soothing, it made me shed a tear. The acknowledgment and celebration of love and marriage were beautiful. From the tears of marrying the love of your life to the joy of spending the rest of your life with them. Almost every meme included was hilarious and adorable like the young girl who has a prosthetic leg and her classmates were excited to see her. I enjoyed the part about the Black activists and public figures who made an impact and who paved the way for all of us. Furthermore, I would like to thank you Mr. Joseph. Thank you for sharing your creativity and art with us. Thank you for bringing me tears of joy, knowledge, and laughter. Thank you for giving me another person to be inspired by, which is you.

Sincerely,
Kenise Brown

Dear Kahlil Joseph,
As a student at New Jersey City University, I've had the opportunity to be exposed to your work. Your ongoing piece, *BLKNWS* impacted me greatly, helping me feel represented and touching parts of me I didn't know existed. It was beautiful to see something so avant-garde, yet so contemporary. It was beautiful to see so many sections of the Black diaspora represented; you've got the range! Black love is not just represented as hetero. It accepts queerness and trans and drag Black love. *BLKNWS* is something I would recommend to any and every college student, but especially Black students in media/art mediums.

Thank you, Kahlil. You've awoken something in me that I never knew was asleep.

Best Regards,
Bianca Paulino

Dear Kahlil Joseph,
Our professor, Vera Dika, showed us an episode of *BLKNWS* in class. It was thought-provoking and had the whole class discussing what interpretations and feelings they got from it, which were all very different from one another. It was nice to see us all be so verbal since it's not always like that. I personally enjoyed the segment about the Uncanny Valley. Humans have feelings of disturbance

when confronted by people and things that are similar to them in appearance—but aren't convincingly close. Since you included Lil Miquela in the video, I took this to mean how people portray themselves over social media in ways different from what they really are. The final product can be a highly edited and not a genuine self. I think the Uncanny Valley was a metaphor for how people get weirded out by people who are different from them in sexual orientation, color, or appearance. It got me thinking about these things. I just wanted to write down my thanks to the *BLKNWS* team and to Kahlil Joseph for allowing my class to see an episode. It opened our eyes and let us find deeper meanings into these images.

All Best,
Linnett Oliveras

From my perspective, I understand that *BLKNWS* has invited white viewers to enter a black subject position.[7] I found that I recognized some of the personalities and references presented, but not others. I am familiar with Maya Angelou and Cornel West, for example, and I could acknowledge Angelou's discussion of the strength of black women,

7 Arthur Jafa, "In Your Face", interviewed by Carrie Scott, *SHOWStudio*, publ. November 24, 2017, video, 52:13, https://www.youtube.com/watch?v=XAkOdkOlAWw. Jafa discusses how black audiences have been traditionally asked to see the world in media from a white subject position. In *BLKNWS*, and in Jafa's own work, such *Love is the Message, the Message is Death*, the situation is reversed. The white viewer is invited into a black subject position to see from a different world perspective.

and the historically convulsive fact that black women have "nurtured generations of white strangers." And while I could not have named the musician DC Young Fly or the comedian Charlie Che Matters, I could sympathize with what Matters meant in his comedy routine when he repeated, with differing inflections, the slogan "Black lives *matter ... simply ... matter ...*" noting that this was a rather "low bar to start the negotiations." I did recall, however, Steven Spielberg's *Amistad* and the scene where the young mother on the slave ship tips backwards and falls overboard while holding her baby in her arms. I remembered originally being saddened and shocked by this moment in Spielberg's film, but seeing it again in the context of *BLKNWS*, and hearing the responses of my students, brought me to a different level of awareness. The scene on the slave ship in *BLKNWS* is followed by a satellite shot of the oceans of the earth. The feeling of being engulfed, submerged in its vastness was palpable, but then intensified when one of my students, a young mother of a six-month old child, began to cry and said she would do the same rather have her son live in slavery.

BLKNWS's aim is to allow an exchange between the speaker and listeners, like a graffiti scrawl, and to raise awareness to resist the dominant powers that work to subjugate a people. The "people" here can be seen to refer specifically to the black community, and to other marginalized ethnic or gender groups, and the political, social and economic challenges that face them. But by implication, *BLKNWS* also calls for all viewers imbricated in the media's system of control and irresponsibility to acknowledge the need for a mutual exchange in all forms of communication.

Mirroring in a Movie: Or on Community Feeling Taking Shape in Vittorio De Seta and Éric Baudelaire

Malvina Borgherini

"I'm so happy when my aunt arrives from abroad ... When I see her I laugh, and feel my tummy flutter like roses in the wind." That was the delicate metaphor articulated by Alaa Al-Asaad, a little boy originally from Acre yet growing up in Burj Al-Barajneh refugee camp, upon his rare brush with a world of grace and kindness. And it is quite emblematic that this metaphor was chosen as title for a volume that accumulated the creative activities of a group of children, fourth generation Palestinian refugees living in Lebanon.[1] Looking carefully in the mirror, observing through a lens the eyes that allow others to see you, trying to describe yourself in words as well as through drawing; these were some of the activities put to the children by Laila Kanafani in the camp on the southern outskirts of Beirut. It was part of an educational project by the Ghassan Kanafani Cultural Foundation.[2] Struck by Loris Malaguzzi's

1 Laila Ghassan Kanafani, *Like Roses in the Wind: Self-Portraits and Thoughts* (Beirut: Ghassan Kanafani Cultural Foundation, 2003).

2 GKCF is an NGO founded by Anni Høver (together with some friends, subsequently with her children Fayez and Laila) on July 8, 1974, the second

methodology as practiced by Italian kindergartens in Reggio Emilia,[3] Laila managed to rekindle the poetry and political endeavor of her late father—assassinated in 1974—by launching a training program for children that transforms the experience of self-portraiture into an awareness of one's own identity as a basis from which to start to understand the world.[4] As an individual or as a group, in emancipating the person and the community and as an essential resource towards a plural and respectful coexistence, self-awareness is a social and political condition. Its representation (by a third party) of a community, or its self-representation, seems to make that immediately obvious.

When Vittorio De Seta began to film bodies and record sounds and songs in southern Italy during the

anniversary of the death of her husband Ghassan Kanafani (Acre 1936–Beirut 1972), a writer, poet, journalist and political activist in the Popular Front for the Liberation of Palestine (PFLP), assassinated in an attack organized by Mossad.

3 Laila Kanafani, graduated in art from the University of Beirut, founded the GKCF art and creativity project for nursery schools and educational centers in Palestinian refugee camps as well as disadvantaged areas in Lebanon. The idea originated from a seminar she attended in Reggio Emilia, Italy, a city renowned as a nexus of pedagogical practices, highly influenced by the life and work of Loris Malaguzzi (Correggio 1920–Reggio Emilia 1994). "Education is a right for everyone, for girls and boys and as such it is a responsibility of the community. Education is an opportunity for growth and emancipation of the individual and the community, it is a resource for knowledge and coexistence, it is a meeting ground where freedom, democracy, solidarity are practiced and peace as a value is promoted. Within the plurality of cultural, ideological, political and religious conceptions, education thrives on listening, dialogue and participation; it is aimed at respecting and enhancing diverse identities, skills, knowledge, of which each individual is the bearer and therefore qualifies as a lay person, open to contrast and cooperation" (from *Infant and Nursery Schools Regulations* of Reggio Emilia's city council).

4 Manuela De Leonardis, "Gli occhi dei bambini vedono meglio," *Il Manifesto*, January 8, 2020, https://ilmanifesto.it/gli-occhi-dei-bambini-vedono-meglio.

1950s, in territories where men, women and children were united by the hard daily struggle for survival, he could not yet foresee exactly where that experience might lead him, but he had the clear-cut desire to merge with that environment and to allow for a sort of mediated self-representation.

> I was studying architecture and had always been attracted to cinema [...] In the end I threw myself in and made Il pescespada [*Lu tempu di lu pisci spata*] 35mm, in color. I went with a guy, Alfredo Manganiello, who helped me carry the stuff. But I was alone: either shooting, or recording; indeed the sound is not in sync. I remember throwing myself around without knowing what I would do with those scenes ... there wasn't a script, there wasn't any lengthy preparation, there was just this idea of merging with the environment, of being part of the environment, to build the work going along. In the evening I just listened to the tapes because I couldn't see the scenes in playback. And so I built the documentary as we worked, in contact with reality. I knew nothing about the people, I wasn't familiar with them [...] But in captivity I had known—looking back—the working people, and for me it had a decisive effect because I understood things about relationships, the bonds of friendship.[5] So when I started making documentaries I thought of filming ordinary

5 Vittorio De Seta was interned in a concentration camp near Salzburg between 1943 and 1945.

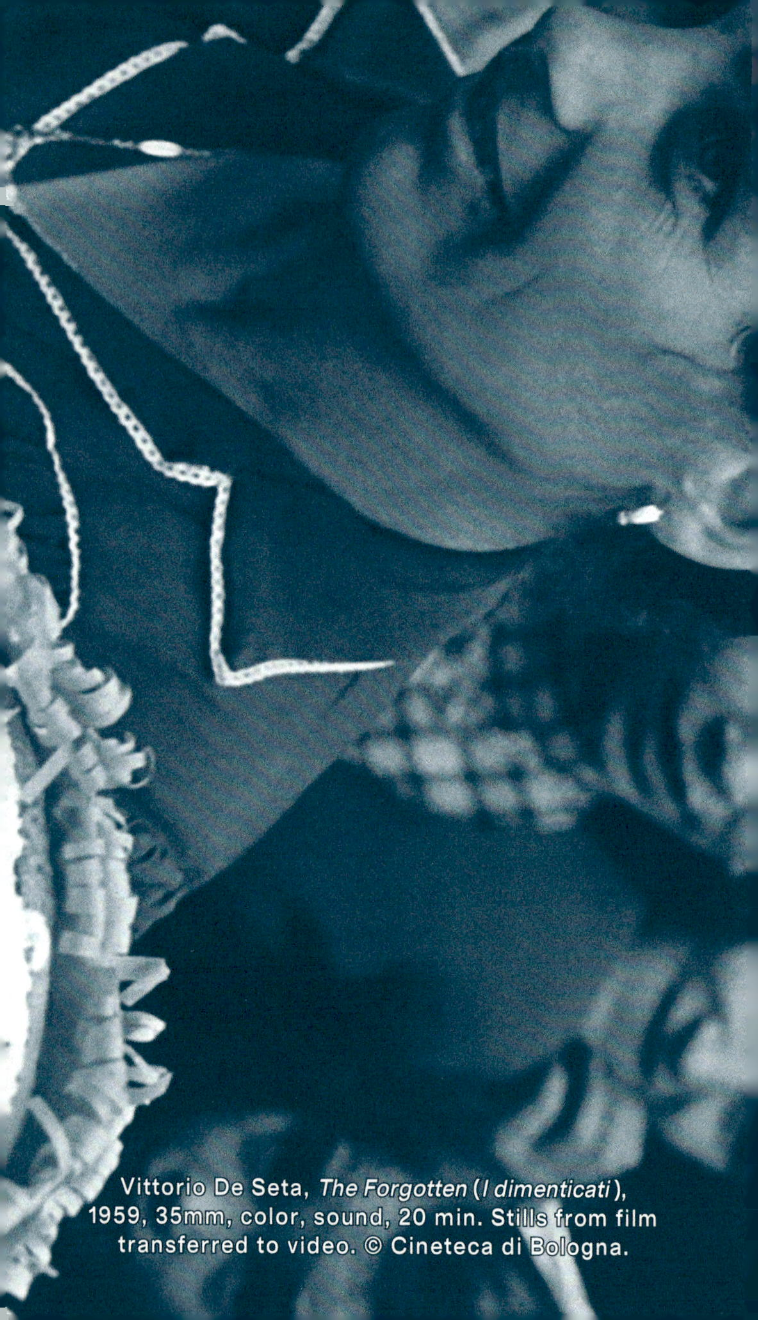

Vittorio De Seta, *The Forgotten* (*I dimenticati*), 1959, 35mm, color, sound, 20 min. Stills from film transferred to video. © Cineteca di Bologna.

> people at work in Sicily, but without having an overt premonition that all this way of life would disappear within a few years. One felt it, one presented it, yet it seemed impossible ...[6]

In his series of ten short films shot around Sicily, Sardinia and Calabria between 1954 to 1959,[7] De Seta observes and shows the everyday deeds of fishermen, farm workers, miners and shepherds, those who live a visceral existence with the land and sea. He listens to and relays individual voices, whose singularity exists through being part of a whole. It brings to light and renders an archaic culture recognizable, laying itself bare to see through its expressive ways.

Every scene shot in Alessandria del Carretto, an inaccessible mountain village where the protagonists of *The Forgotten* (*I dimenticati*) live, is quite choral: from the transportation of supplies by men with mules, traversing fifteen kilometers of crags and streams, on to the expected arrival in the village, during which the elderly, women and children join the long caravan, following it with their gaze from niches along the stoney streets; from the felling, dragging and final adorning of a tall fir trunk that, through exertion imbued with glee, is raised up as a Cockaigne

6 From an interview by Gian Luca Farinelli of Vittorio De Seta. Reproduced as *Supplément: Entretien avec Vittorio De Seta* (18 min.), in *Vittorio De Seta: Le monde perdu. Le regard sur le Sud de l'Italie des anées 50*, DVD, color, 101 min. (Bologna: Carlotta Films-Cineteca di Bologna, 2008).

7 *Lu tempu di li pisci spata* (1954, 11 min.), *Isola di fuoco* (1954, 11 min.), *Sulfarara* (1955,10 min.), *Pasqua in Sicilia* (1955, 11 min.), *Contadini del mare* (1955, 10 min.), *Parabola d'oro* (1955, 10 min.), *Pescherecci* (1958, 11 min.), *Pastori di Orgosolo* (1958, 11 min.), *Un giorno in Barbagia* (1958, 14 min.), *I dimenticati* (1959, 20 min.).

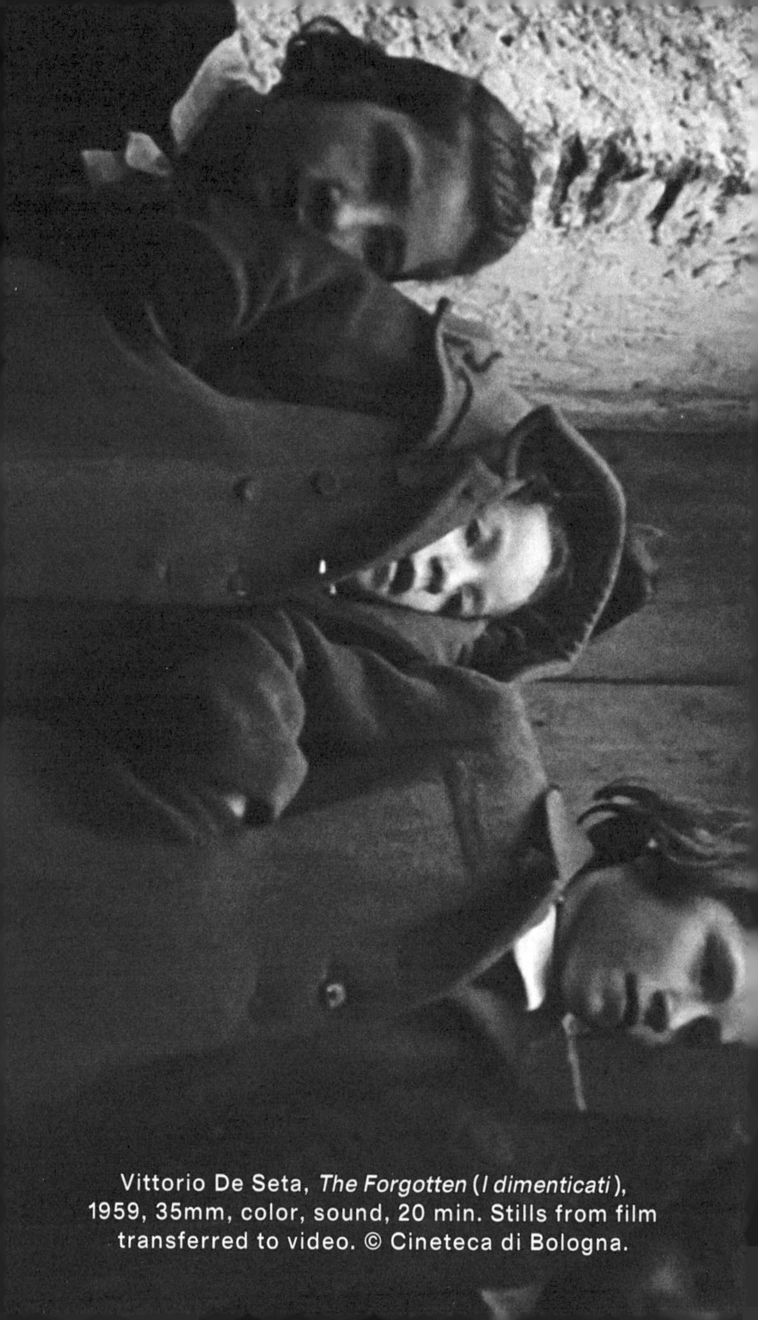

Vittorio De Seta, *The Forgotten* (*I dimenticati*), 1959, 35mm, color, sound, 20 min. Stills from film transferred to video. © Cineteca di Bologna.

pole at the entrance of the village, to a man shinning-up and conquering its heights, with his subsequent tossing down of braided bread and necklaces of figs to the whole community that throngs around that tall tree of plenty like an embrace; from the auction of cheeses or saplings decorated with candy that had been fashioned by the womenfolk to pay for the celebrations, to the great feast where everyone gathers around long tablecloths laid out on the grass.

The moments of collective festivities in Alessandria del Carretto in which De Seta participates—the welcome of the arrival of the supplies, the spring festival with the careening tree trunk—give shape to a portrait of the *body in common*, in which everyday activities coexist with ritual festivities of a thousand-year-old culture and the indelible physical signs of the harshness of that existence. A community that in its mirroring in a movie assumes a self-awareness of its deepest essence.

> The country folk, the fishermen, were not aware of having a culture. This struck me, because when I was leaving they asked me what I came for, what is here? As if to say there's nothing here. What is this film? But when I brought the documentary to them, when I sent *The Forgotten to Alexandria*—at the time they only released two or three copies of the film—they didn't want to give it back to me anymore. Watching the documentary, they realized that theirs was a culture, there had been this element of unawareness; all places had a name,

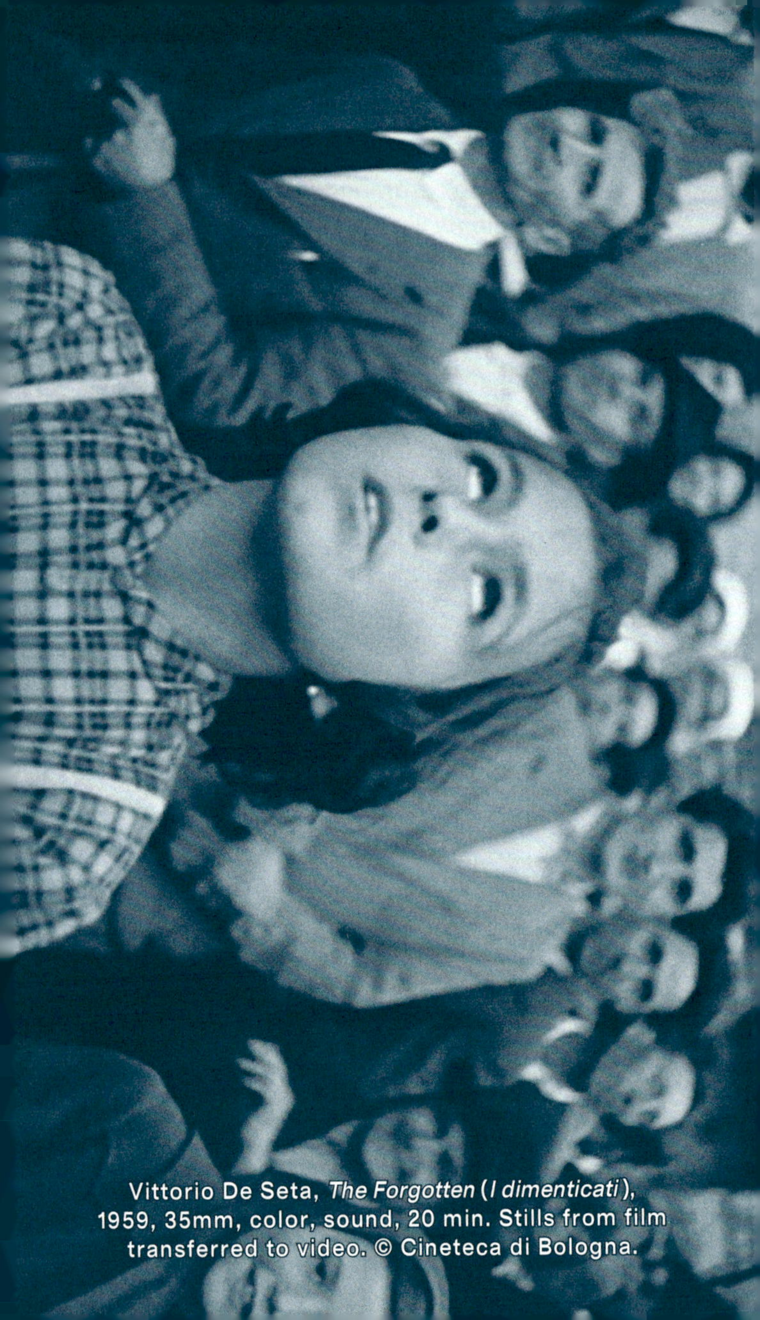

Vittorio De Seta, *The Forgotten* (*I dimenticati*), 1959, 35mm, color, sound, 20 min. Stills from film transferred to video. © Cineteca di Bologna.

almost always sacred names, the territory itself was alive, all life was punctuated with these rites, these liturgies, these songs.[8]

Sixty years later and over to the French side of the Alps, there is another world,[9] one with its communities in the process of growth or risk of extinction, and this is also mirrored in a movie. This is Éric Baudelaire's most recent film, an authored work and choral work at the same time.

Un film dramatique, financed by a percentage of state funds (allocated by French law for every public building in the form of an art commission)[10] takes shape as a sort of intangible growth of the Dora Maar middle school in banlieue Saint-Denis, northern Paris. Shown at the Center Pompidou as one part of Éric Baudelaire's three-part project *Tu peux prendre ton temps*, the film ends up increasing the value of the structure by relocating it to the center (during the exhibition the school is visible and fully functioning

8 De Seta, interview.

9 Unfortunately there is no room here to detail the complexity and diversity of the contemporary scene, the transformations wrought over these last few decades in which communication, in the face of a series of "miraculous and traumatic" events, contemporarily takes the place of an individual and collective. Cf. regarding Mario Perniola, *Miracoli e trauma della comunicazione* (Torino: Einaudi, 2009) and Jean Baudrillard, *Per una critica dell'economia politica del segno* (Milano: Mimesis, 2010) orig. pub. *Pour une critique de l'economie politique du signe*, (Paris: Éditions Gallimard, 1972).

10 Under one French edict, commonly known as "1% Artistique" (decree no. 2002-677 of April 29, 2002), it stipulates the inclusion of an original work of art in every public building project (usually an object, often a sculpture) which thus becomes an integral part of the architecture, allocating one percent of the amount set aside for construction to a living artist. The aim of this legislation was to sensitize public opinion to contemporary art, its initial formulation dates back to 1983.

in the heart of Paris),[11] as well as becoming part of an active process in developing awareness for a community of kids from a Parisian banlieue.

You Can Take Your Time, was not only the title of that Pompidou installation, nor just an adroit supplication to its visitors, it was rather an expression of what Baudelaire actually granted himself and to all those who participated with him in the project. Over the past four years the director—who hails from a political science background—regularly met with a group of Dora Maar schoolchildren with whom he ceaselessly interrogated, asking them about what type of thing they planned to make together (Was this a documentary? A fiction film? Perhaps a drama?) as well as enquiring about their own lives and what was happening around them at the time.[12]

The sequence of activities that the director nurtured within the school only somewhat corresponds to the sequences in the final film. Before having video equipment and microphones entrusted into their own hands, the kids had interrogated themselves and discussed ideas for a whole year, issuing from

11 The collective exhibition *Prix Marcel Duchamp 2019, Les Nommés*, attended by the artists Éric Baudelaire, Katinka Bock, Marguerite Humeau, Ida Tursic & Wilfried Mille, was held from October 9, 2019, to January 6, 2020, for the Marcel Duchamp award, won by Baudelaire himself. The installation *Tu peux prendre ton temps* was composed of three works: two were shown inside the Pompidou, *Un film dramatique* (114 min.) and the short film *Prélude* (13 min.) while the third required relocating to Saint-Denis (where, on the top of Tour Pleyel, in front of Collège Dora Maar, some pupils there who had also co-authored the film, along with the artist Daniel Buren, had hoisted a flag).

12 Among the most significant events were the Islamic fundamentalist terrorist attacks that shook France throughout 2015: the most egregious of these occurring on November 13, in and around the nearby Bataclan theatre, murdering well over a hundred people.

questions posed by Baudelaire; completely autonomously, over the next three years, they began to explore their surroundings by placing themselves in each other's gaze, listening to others or trying to observe themselves via their reflection in the eye of a lens. In this timespan—relatively brief in the course of a lifetime, rather long for the production of any film—their bodies grew, their voices altered, their experiences had been stratified, the recordings had took the form of personal archives. This acquired distancing has allowed them to see themselves as a community, as forms of life within relationships.

The film opens with an attempt to film a bright dot in the night sky. "What's that, a star? It's not a plane, it doesn't move ..." demands an off-screen voice, whilst trying to focus on the mysterious object, adjusting the video camera's zoom. The noise of this enlarged image, shot in semi-darkness, generates a stippling of other dots—around the brighter, clearly oscillating one, which the camera's eye tries in vain to stabilize—becoming a sort of digital vault of heaven. And superimposed upon this novel celestial firmament are the names of the project's authors, appearing in scattered order, like so many stars: Poullet-Malassis Films (the production company's name is a nod to Charles Baudelaire's publisher, a tie-in with the director's namesake), Éric Baudelaire, the children's names and the editor Claire Atherton.

Such a constellation of names is a clear statement on the idea of authorship, dear to Baudelaire. It shows a process in its becoming, from object of creation to subject, which, beginning to

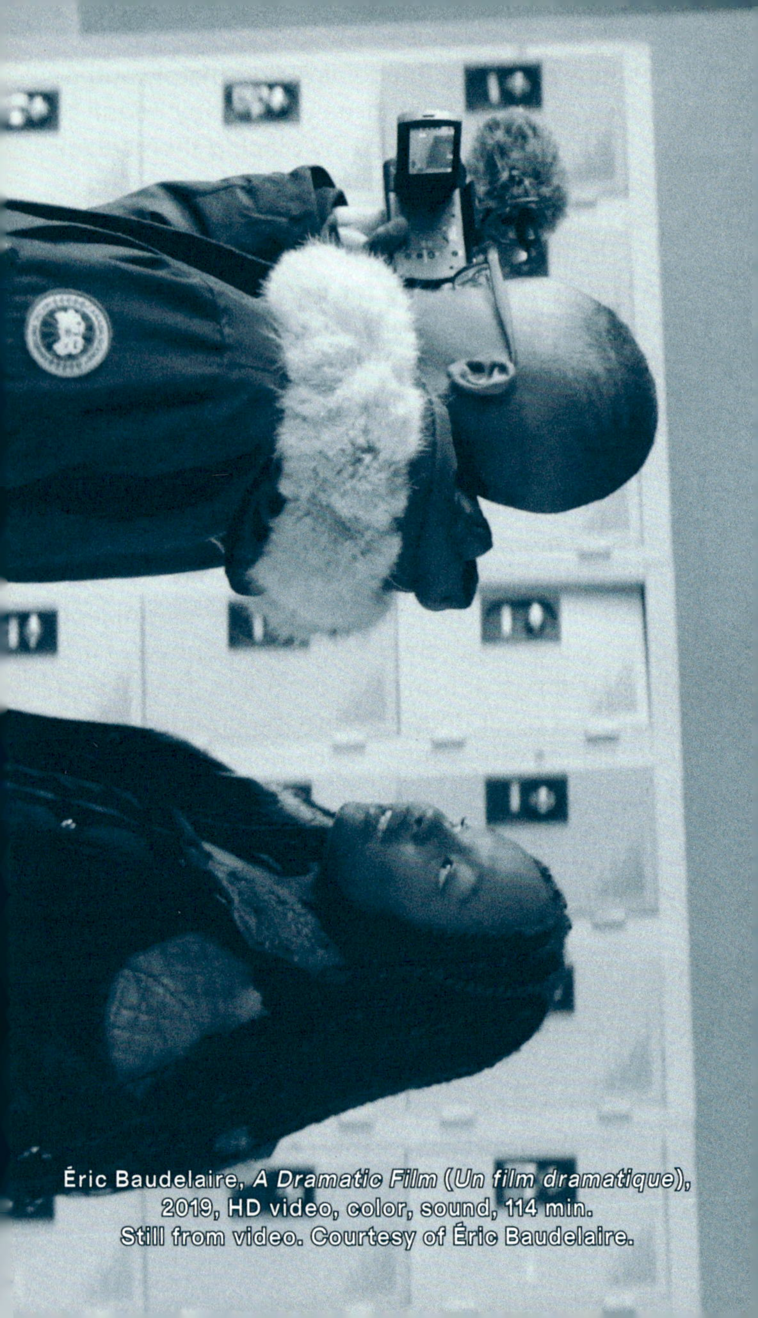

Éric Baudelaire, *A Dramatic Film* (*Un film dramatique*), 2019, HD video, color, sound, 114 min. Still from video. Courtesy of Éric Baudelaire.

consciously assume itself as such, enters into the role of co-authorship of the work. A process that requires time and distance—which are generated between one moment and another, where stories settle, experiences mature, bodies transform, in an assembly that creates a political subject and emerges as an artwork—just like those required self-glances, done in order to make one accessible to others, while they become co-authors of a film and subjects of their own lives.

Youthful voices can be heard while the screen remains dark, arguing with each other about what a film can be—"it can be about anything ... it is a moving story, a moving fairy tale"—then finally the first trembling images, shot in the street outside the school: as if the building, itself absorbed into the unsullied gaze of a child, opened its eyes in front of itself. And then, a little later, this time to observe (and also name, as a voice lists them) the multiplicity of identities that constitute this surroundings: a Chinese diner, a Pakistani and Indian restaurant, a Greek grill, a bar brasserie, a grocery and a bakery, metro and bus stops, and above all a skyscraper awaiting demolition to make way for a hotel.

Exchanges of gazes that shape that political subject, which could imply architecture too if understood as a community, as an organization of spaces with people in a mutual relationship; starting from that idea of constructing the political subject which Baudelaire had been exploring for some time, drawing on the landscape theory of revolutionary film director Masao Adachi: "a good way of under-

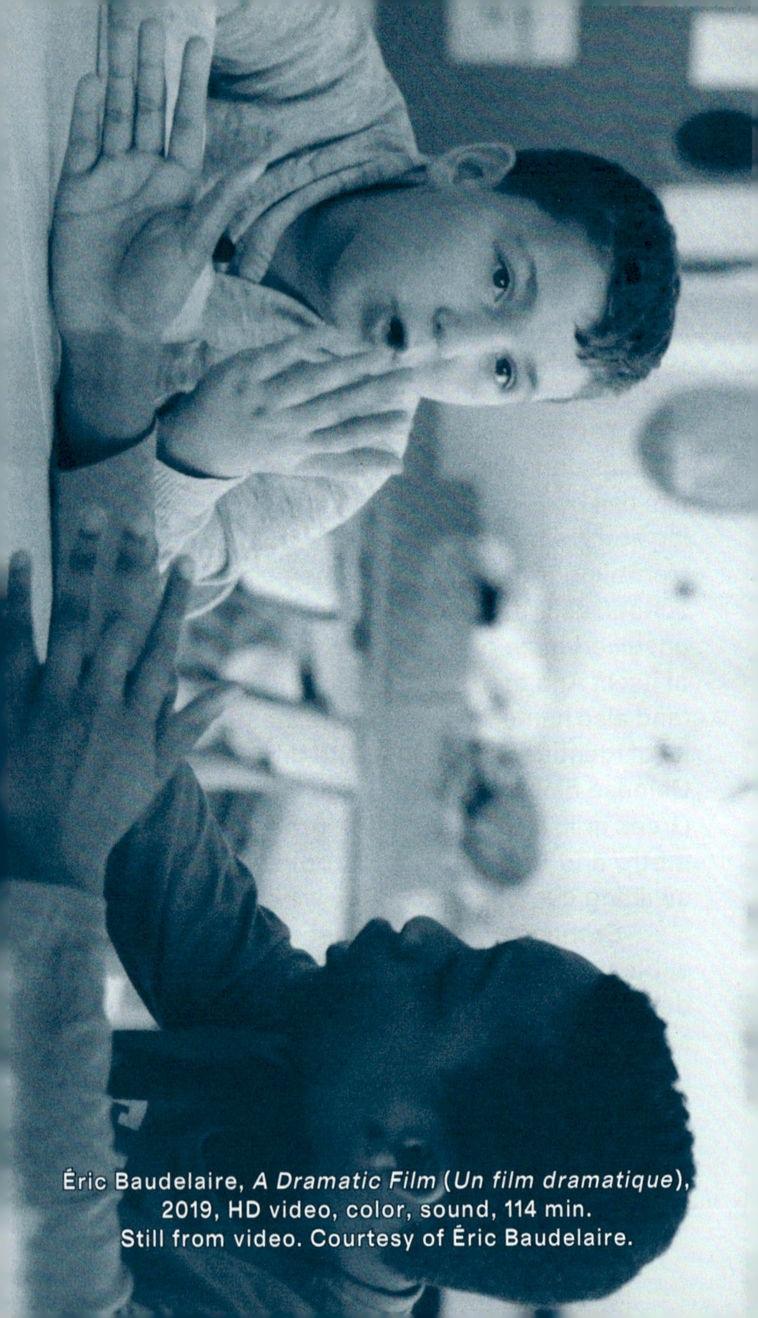

Éric Baudelaire, *A Dramatic Film* (*Un film dramatique*), 2019, HD video, color, sound, 114 min. Still from video. Courtesy of Éric Baudelaire.

standing someone is to look at what they see."[13]

In another scene two kids introduce themselves to us inside the school: one speaks, describing in real time what the other is filming, while from another point of view, like any external spectator, a camera follows them, watching and listening in on them. A quick glance from the two boys, asking for confirmation about what path to follow, goes right beyond the viewer's gaze and swops with that of the director.

It is not only the children's bodies that change, while we follow them during their initial group discussions, then their individual self-portraits; the look in their eyes changes too, at first excited and in need of direction, by the end they seem more proud and aware, through those exchanges with one another or through mirroring themselves in a video camera in order to study themselves more deeply. In the first scenes we see the group in various configurations, discussing the project, current affairs (initiated in the wake of the harrowing terrorist attacks), their different identities (each child's family having diverse origins, even though all felt French first and foremost) and the forms of discrimination they encountered—Why are all the inhabitants of a

13 Philippe Mangeot, "Éric Baudelaire," in *Le Prix Marcel Duchamp 2019: Éric Baudelaire, Katinka Boch, Marguerite Humeau, Ida Tursic & Wilfried Mille* (Milano: Silvana Editoriale, 2019), 17, (extract from the Centre Pompidou exhibition catalogue, October 9, 2019–January 6, 2020). Masao Adachi, prominent exponent of the art and literary counterculture of the 1960s and 70s, he spent a large part of his life engaged at home as a member of the outlawed Japanese Red Army up until 1971, and then for the Palestinians in George Habash's PFLP faction. He was arrested in Lebanese on February 15, 1997; on March 18, 2000, he was extradited to Japan, where he remained incarcerated until 2003. Today, over seventy years old, he lives freely in Japan but is not allowed to leave the country.

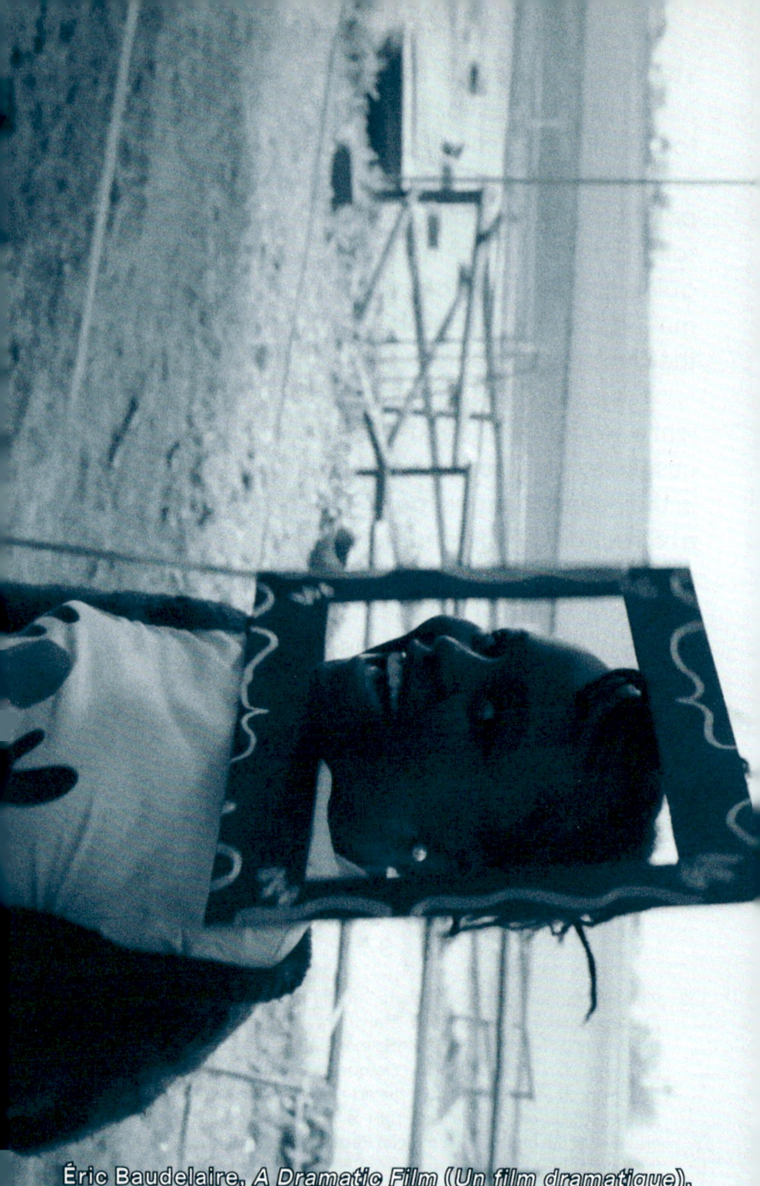

Éric Baudelaire, *A Dramatic Film (Un film dramatique)*, 2019, HD video, color, sound, 114 min. Still from video. Courtesy of Éric Baudelaire.

banlieue deemed to be violent?"—yet we also see them reflect, together with the director, on the various elements that make up a film—What is framing, focus? What is the difference between sound and noise? What is synchronization between sound and image?—plus film's different narrative formulas.

Perhaps the most emblematic images of the film are during their experience of creating self-portraits. Images that, condensing four years of life in less than two hours of footage, a sort of extended time-lapse, open the way to growth and to the process that underlies it, towards a wider participation, to a community in the making that is mirrored in a movie.

David is a case in point, he shows up in distant places, at different times: some spent in Romania, in the countryside near his grandmother's house; some spent at the Collège Dora Maar, in the same spot from where the rest of kids talk in front of a video camera, over the years. At first, superimposing ourselves on the camera's eye, we spy a chubby-faced boy who turns to someone off-screen, seeking corroboration for his pronouncements ("A man lived 20 centuries, he was richer than anybody. He left behind his riches, etc. And had some good fights: that can be a film. You can invent ... stuff. A film can be about anything and everything. But it's not like photos, Because photos are of yourself, in the present, but films can invent people who don't exist. Who aren't real"). By the final scenes David has became a pimply teenager who peers at us defiantly, as if reflected in the lens he seeks to stare us out; while at the beginning it was the eyes of the director with whom he spoke, that effectively became his mirror.

The film ends, as it began, at the entrance of the school. And it is as if the building continues to stare back out, following two girls while they express fantasy color schemes and other improvements to Dora Maar.

—Here it'll be ... We'll destroy the bars. Make them black and white (now they are all white a/n). It'll be dope! Black white, black white, black white ...
—Moving on. We'll take the guardhouse away. And we'll put up ...
—A curtain. You just go through it. And then here (they show the outside gate a/n) ... Here, we'll do ... Black white again.
—No, not again. Salmon! A salmon color.
—And here (they look at the facade a/n) ... I don't like it. It should be gold.
—Yes, gold!
—On the ground, here ... Like a red carpet, but in silver.
—And the posts?
—Let's paint them pink tiger stripes. Yeah! Tiger stripe or leopard could be good.
—We'll change this because it's ugly.
—It's all wrong. The grass has to be bright yellow.
—Like the sun ... really yellow!
Yes! I'm not OK with the fence. It has to go with the yellow, like orange or red.
—Right. And there, the gym ...
—Wait, the gym grey.
—Yes! We'll change it, we'll put ... Black on the ground, but the walls?

—White.
—Yes, white.
—And outside?
—The zebra crossing has to stand out.
—Fluorescent.
—Yes! Reflecting all day long. Even the cars will be dazzled!

Although moving through different times and places, as well as in very dissimilar human environments, the works of Baudelaire and De Seta reveal unexpected common features. The community to which Baudelaire opens our participation to is both close, yet at the same time distant, from that which De Seta represents (and introduces us to) in another of his films: *Diary of a Teacher* (Diario di un maestro).[14] It was shot in a school on the outskirts of Rome between April and July 1971. As De Seta himself explains, in recounting the experience of discovering and unveiling another community of forgotten people, the fundamental idea was not so much to make a film, but to make a school and then film it.

14 Produced as a television drama and first broadcast in 1973 on RAI in four episodes, *Diary of a Teacher* is based on Albino Bernardini's autobiography Un anno a Pietralata (Firenze: La nuova Italia, 1968), which chronicles the experience of a teacher in a Roman suburb who had a clear notion of an ideal school, unlike any institutional reality, one that backs the skills and potential of its pupils. The schoolmaster, the actor Bruno Cirino, worked on De Seta's screenplay which soon become a malleable enough canvas to incorporate the reactions and personalities of the children involved. And it is from the latter, those actual inhabitants of the Tiburtino Terzo, Torraccia and Pietralata districts, that the school recreated in the De Seta film arose, originating from Bernardini's experience. For further details see Vittorio De Seta, Federico Rossin, ed., *Diario di un maestro, Journal d'un maître d'école. Le film, un livre* (Paris: L'Arachnéen, 2019).

The traits that seem to unite the two directors arise from their shared interest in the way community feeling takes shape—sought by overlapping the gaze of the other or, conversely, placing oneself in a position to reflect it—in an undefined space on the edges, between the imaginary and reality, between naivety and awareness, between improvisation and authorship.

Biographies

Malvina Borgherini, associate professor of Design, teaches courses in architecture, multimedia arts, theater and performing arts at the Iuav University of Venice, where she is also the scientific director of the MeLa Media Lab and of the master's degree MOVIES—Moving Images Arts. Her area of research has developed around the themes of theory and history of architectural representation, recently focusing on vision and the relationship between representation and image, its shift from the nineteenth century incorporation of the objectivity of the *camera obscura*, to today where it is located within the subjectivity of the human body.

Enrico Camporesi oversees the research and documentation activities at the film collection of the Musée national d'art moderne—Centre Pompidou, where he also conceived and organized several film and video programs. In 2017 he was awarded the first Terra Foundation for American Art postdoctoral fellowship at the Institut national d'histoire de l'art in Paris for a research project on Annette Michelson's work as critic and curator. He is the author of *Futurs de l'obsolescence*, a book on the restoration of experimental and artists' films (Éditions Mimésis, 2018).

Writer, film historian and educator, Vera Dika (Ph.D. in Cinema Studies, New York University) specializes in American mainstream and avant-garde film. She has written for *Artforum* and *Art in America*, is one of the founding editors of *Millennium Film*

Journal, and is the author of *The (Moving) Pictures Generation: New York Downtown Film and Art* (New York: Palgrave Macmillan, 2012), *Recycled Culture in Contemporary Art and Film: the Uses of Nostalgia* Cambridge: Cambridge University Press, 2003).

From 2015 Sibylle de Laurens and Pascaline Morincôme have been leading a research project which explores the alternative video scene in the US. In 2017, within the Parisian exhibition space Treize, they curated an exhibition devoted to the Videofreex collective and had organized several evenings, screenings and lectures in collaboration with The Cheapest University, the École nationale supérieure d'arts de Paris-Cergy and the Parsons School of Art and Design. Meanwhile, they have continued to coordinate Seedy Films, an initiative focused on the links between filmed and printed forms, hosted at the Bibliothèque Kandinsky at the Centre Pompidou. Their 2019 *Seedy Films* program devoted itself to the archives of the alternative art space *EZTV* and its founder John Dorr.

Lorenzo Lazzari researches those relationships between the moving image and politics that are able to reveal the implicit violence of which the objects examined are symbols, testimonies, or conveyors. In 2018 he was a research fellow at the Iuav University of Venice and collaborator at MeLa Media Lab. In 2019 he won the i-Portunus Creative Europe grant and became co-curator of the teaching program of the postgraduate course

MOVIES—Moving Images Arts. He is currently studying towards a Ph.D. in Art History, Film and Media Studies at the University of Udine.

Videofreex, a start-up since 1969, was one of the pioneer indy production groups of early users that formed when consumer video was first introduced. During more than a decade together, the members produced several thousand videotapes, installations and multimedia events, and trained hundreds of video-makers in the brand new medium. They were part of a fast-growing alternative video network that captured many political and social movements and the counter culture. Decades later, the Freex early videotapes serve as a window into this unique era of social and cultural change.

Thanks to the contributors and Éric Baudelaire, Deborah Birch, Skip Blumberg, Guy Borlée, Nancy Cain, Tom Colley, Chiara Davino, Alexandra Delage, Bart Friedman, Davidson Gigliotti, Grafiche Veneziane, Friederike Gratz, Kahlil Joseph, Lorenzo Mason Studio, Hélène Maes, Susanna Maistrello, Abina Manning, Philippe-Alain Michaud, Mary Curtis Ratcliff, Emily Rose, Jim Sunderland, Parry Teasdale, Treize, Videofreex.com, Carol Vontobel.

First edition, 2020

Adriatico Book Club
www.adriaticobook.club

Università Iuav di Venezia
www.iuav.it

Università Iuav di Venezia

This book has been partially funded by i-Portunus
www.i-portunus.eu

i-Portunus

Funded by the Creative Europe Programme of the European Union

With kind support of
MeLa Media Lab, www.mela.iuav.it
MOVIES—Moving Images Arts, www.mov-ies.eu

On Responsibility: The Moving
Image Questions Spectatorship

Publishers: Adriatico Book Club,
Grafiche Veneziane, Università Iuav di Venezia

Editing: Lorenzo Lazzari

Texts: Malvina Borgherini, Enrico Camporesi,
Vera Dika, Sibylle de Laurens, Lorenzo Lazzari,
Pascaline Morincôme, Videofreex
Translations: Jim Sunderland
Proofreading: Deborah Birch, Jim Sunderland

Design and Layout: Lorenzo Mason Studio
Typeface: Peso Medium Informal,
Lorenzo Mason Studio

Paper: Papyrus Terraprint Gloss
Printing and Binding: Grafiche Veneziane
Printed in Venice, Italy

ISBN: 978-88-98488-55-1
978-88-31241-32-8

Adriatico Book Club
www.adriaticobook.club